EASY
OVEN DISHES

Caribbean Roast Pork, page 46

EASY
OVEN DISHES

RODALE

Cover photograph: Mitch Mandel
Cover recipe: Curried Chicken Potpie
Courtesy of McCormick, page 75
Food stylist: Diane Vezza
Illustrations: Judy Newhouse

Editorial produced by:
BETH ALLEN ASSOCIATES, INC.

President/Owner: Beth Allen
Culinary Consultant/Food Editor: Deborah Mintcheff
Project Editors: Stephanie Avidon, Melissa Moritz
Recipe Editor: Jackie Mills
Nutritionist: Michele C. Fisher, Ph.D., R.D.
Art Production Director: Laura Smyth (smythtype)
Photo Researcher: Valerie Vogel

Library of Congress Cataloging-in-Publication Data

Easy oven dishes.
       p.   cm.
   Includes index.
   ISBN-13 978–1–59486–146–8 hardcover
   ISBN-10 1–59486–146–3 hardcover
    1. Casserole cookery.   2. Quick and easy cookery. I. Rodale (Firm)
  TX693.E183 2005
  641.8'21—dc22   2004023641

2 4 6 8 10 9 7 5 3   hardcover

We inspire and enable people to improve their lives and the world around them

For more of our products visit **rodalestore.com** or call 800-848-4735

CONTENTS

INTRODUCTION

The best kitchen helper you can have

Remember those Sunday dinners at Grandma's? She never looked happier than when she took a roasted chicken out of the oven—golden, crispy, juicy, and bursting with her moist bread stuffing. Twice-baked potatoes and her buttermilk biscuits were soon to follow. Just when you didn't think you could eat another bite, out came a cherry pie baked that morning and topped as always with a perfectly woven lattice made of the flakiest pastry in the world. There always seemed to be something scrumptious and heavenly coming out of her oven—forever stirred up and served with lots of love and care. The same comforting foods that created those delicious memories are exactly what this book is all about.

Easy Oven Dishes is just what the title promises: delicious oven-baked dishes that are easy to put together and bake on their own, with little help from you. Expect to find many of your favorites, such as Stuffed Pork Chops (page 50), Oven-Fried Honey Chicken (page 68), and Boston Baked Beans (page 113)—all with that incredible down-home flavor, yet made easier and faster. Plus, there are fresh twists on many classics, including serving roasted vegetables with meat loaf, cooking chicken in convenient foil packets, and flavoring homemade chicken potpie with Indian curry and other good flavors.

Who can resist a plate of Mom's Mac & Cheese (page 31) made with plenty of mild and sharp Cheddars? Or a supper of finger-lickin' Honey-Glazed Spareribs (page 52), roasted under a spicy honey-chili sauce, or a thick slice of Apricot-Glazed Ham (page 45), with its spicy-sweet brown sugar and apricot nectar glaze? All of the oven recipes in this collection come to you with an added surprise: Many use convenience foods, shortcut tips, and easy chef's techniques to capture great homemade taste but often in much less time than your grandmother ever dreamed possible. Like all Quick Cook recipes, each takes 30 minutes (or less!) to mix and make. Many are ready for the oven in only 5 or 10 minutes. Just slide the dish into the oven, walk away, and come back to a juicy pot roast, a cheesy pasta bake, a platter of oven-fried chicken, or a shrimp pie. While in the oven, the flavors blend together to bring back memories of those home-cooked foods every time you take a bite. It's no-fuss, no-worry cooking at its great-tasting best!

Begin rediscovering the treasures your oven has to offer by just turning this page and reading about "Easy-Does-It Cooking." Find out how a simple bag or piece of foil can become an individual cooking vessel, steaming and blending the flavors of dishes like Pineapple Chicken Packets (page 73) in ways you never thought possible. Discover the subtle but oh-so-important flavoring that a mirepoix (that's a French term for the simple mix of fresh carrots, celery, and onion) can add to the roasting pan. Then choose one of the quick chops to make for tonight's dinner. (They're cut so thin they're done in half the time!)

For more fast supper ideas, look for the *SuperQuick* label, such as the one found next to Salmon with Tomatoes, Spinach & Mushrooms (page 82) in the "Fisherman's Specials" chapter. Any recipe carrying that label goes from shopping bag to table in just 30 minutes or less (the salmon takes only 20!).

Easy Oven Dishes is all made possible thanks to the talented food experts at Rodale who have teamed up with test kitchens and food professionals, plus cooking pros and food manufacturers across the country who all have one goal in mind: to bring you a delicious collection of roasting, braising, and baking dishes that come out of your oven cooked to perfection time after time. There's much more tucked in too. Look for *On the Menu* ideas for what to serve with 3-Cheese Manicotti on page 21, and find some scrumptious ways to make great Scalloped Potatoes from other cooks just like you in the *Cook to Cook* feature on page 102. Check out the *Time Savers* on page 27 for some do-ahead tips when preparing the oven dishes. Someday when you have a little extra time, turn to the *Food Facts* on page 23 to read about the history of the casserole and why it's here to stay! Then head right into the kitchen and bake the delicious Cheesy Ham & Noodle Casserole (page 27) for supper.

All of these tried and true (as well as new) creations that your oven has in store for you are included in *Easy Oven Dishes*. And don't forget that there are many other books in The Quick Cook series which will be coming your way soon. Each one has its own wonderful collection of everything you're looking for in today's cookbooks—great-tasting and quick-cooking recipes, beautiful photographs, and plenty of never-fail tips and techniques.

So turn on your oven right now and begin re-creating those wonderful memories of home-baked foods from Grandma's oven—quicker, easier, and with less effort than she ever could have imagined.

Snapper Veracruz, page 86

Easy-Does-It Cooking!

Nothing could be easier! Brown a few chops, top with a sliced onion and a few seasonings, and slide it all into the oven to finish cooking. Come back later to supper, hot out of the oven. That's the glory of oven cooking. You walk away and food turns into delectable goodness, without any more help from you. Seasonings and spices permeate the food as it cooks. The natural fats in meats and poultry melt to create juicy, tender entrées with juicy flavor in every bite. The natural sugars in vegetables caramelize into deep, flavorful side dishes, and ripe fruits bake into delicious desserts such as cobblers and crisps. Oven cooking is versatile cooking at its finest. It's centuries old but suddenly it's new again, bringing you the best-tasting home-cooked food, as easy as 1-2-3!

OVEN COOKING—THE HIGHS AND LOWS OF IT ALL

Homemakers were delighted when the first thermostatically controlled ovens came on the market around 1915. Finally, they could put a cake in to bake and walk away—without worrying. Ovens were a real help then—and still are today.

When you put food into the oven, the heated dry air surrounds the food and cooks it. Sugars caramelize, natural fats in meats melt away and leave them tender and juicy, and cakes rise high, light, and moist.

Here's a rundown of everything you need to know to make your oven the workhorse of all your kitchen efforts.

FAST AS A FLASH

When you're roasting chicken or meat, the external fat surrounding the meat or in the skin of the bird caramelizes into fabulous flavor, provided the temperature is hot enough. Some chefs recommend searing meat for about 15 minutes at a high heat, just until the skin or external fat browns and turns crusty. The heat is then lowered to what is recommended in the recipe. The lower temperature melts the internal fat, making the meat juicy and full of flavor.

OVEN BRAISING Take a tip from some of the leading restaurant chefs. Whenever braising meats such as a pot roast, use both the top of the stove and the oven. Brown meat on top of the stove first in a Dutch oven or deep pot. Then pour in a little liquid (such as beef stock flavored with red wine) and cover the pot tightly. Put it into the oven for the final cooking, instead of finishing it on top of the stove. The steady, reliable heat of the oven surrounds the meat, allowing it to simmer to juicy, fork-tender perfection. If the braising is completed on top of the stove, the direct heat (which is hard to regulate) can cook the meat before it has time to tenderize. The side of the roast on the bottom of the skillet is likely to overcook and dry out before the roast is tender. And since meat cooks faster on top of the stove than in the oven, there's less time for the meat to tenderize or the flavors to layer and develop.

Braising also works great with steaks! Just sear them fast in a skillet. Then drizzle with a little wine or beef stock, cover, and slide the skillet into a moderate oven for a few minutes to finish cooking.

GIVE YOUR OVEN A CHECKUP!

Even the best and newest ovens need a regular checkup. So be sure to keep a working thermometer in your oven. Place or hang one on the center rack, preferably as close to the center as possible. To check the temperature in your oven, set the oven dial (or digital setting) to a moderate temperature, such as 375°F, and let the oven preheat for about 15 minutes. Now check out the temperature reading on the thermometer. Ideally, it should be 5 (at the most 10) degrees higher or lower than the oven dial. If it's off, check your manual, as you can calibrate some ovens yourself. If not, call a repairman to calibrate it for you.

THE OVEN PROBES

How smart this thermometer is! An oven probe sounds when it's time to take out the roast. The display screen, which remains outside the oven, is sleek and compact and simple to read—usually large digital numbers. There's a

---

Cooking Basics

5 EASY DINNER CHOPS FROM THE OVEN

Here's supper, right out of the kitchens of some of the best restaurant chefs, where the technique of oven braising (see page 10) chops until fork-tender and delicious is embraced.

Here's how: First, brown 4 loin or bone-in rib pork chops (7 to 8 ounces each) in a hot skillet on top of the stove in 1 tablespoon butter and 1 tablespoon oil. Now add the liquid and other extras (see below), cover the skillet tightly, and slide it into a moderate oven to cook until the juices are no longer pink. Serve them hot, right out of the skillet.

LEMON-GLAZED CHOPS
Season chops with lemon-pepper seasoning. Brown them as above, then pour 1 cup of lemonade over the chops and top with thin slices

from 1 large lemon. Cover tightly and cook at 350°F for 20 minutes, or until the juices are no longer pink.

CHOPS WITH APPLE AND CALVADOS Season chops with pumpkin pie seasoning. Brown chops as above, pour 1 cup apple cider and then 2 to 3 tablespoons apple brandy (Calvados) over them. Cover tightly and cook at 350°F for 20 minutes, or until the juices are no longer pink.

PORK CHOPS ITALIANO
Season chops with dried Italian herbs. Brown chops as above, then pour one 14½-ounce can diced tomatoes with garlic and onion (undrained) over the chops and sprinkle with 1 cup shredded mozzarella cheese. Cover tightly and cook at 350°F for 20 minutes,

or until the juices are no longer pink and the cheese melts. Sprinkle with slivered fresh basil.

TEX-MEX CHOPS Sprinkle chops with seasoning salt. Brown chops as above, then pour 1½ cups salsa over the chops and sprinkle with 1 cup shredded Monterey Jack cheese. Cover tightly and cook at 350°F for 20 minutes, or until the juices are no longer pink and the cheese melts. Sprinkle with chopped fresh cilantro.

CRANBERRY CHOPS Season chops with salt and ground white pepper. Brown chops as above, then pour 1 cup cranberry juice cocktail over them and sprinkle with ½ cup dried cherries. Cover tightly and cook at 350°F for 20 minutes, or until the juices are no longer pink.

Oven Roasted Potatoes, page 100

Bacon Cheddar Puffs, page 58

Banana Gingerbread Bars, page 136

probe attached to it with a metal cord. Insert the probe into the center of the meat (not touching the bone) and close the oven door. Punch in the thermometer setting that matches up to the type of meat and doneness you prefer (check the directions). Some of these thermometers let you program in two settings, such as 10 degrees before the meat is ready to take out of the oven and when it's done. Others have a third setting and ways to preset the temperature for different types of meat. When using this thermometer, keep the oven door shut—an alert will sound when the temperature of the meat reaches the degree of doneness. It's time to look at the roast!

BARDING & LARDING

Many roasts are lean and arrive at the meat counter trimmed of much of their fat. But let's face it: Fat's good for a roast! Lean roasts benefit from being wrapped in fat or stuffed with a little fat to help prevent them from drying out and becoming tough. Here are two traditional methods for getting that extra-lean roast ready for the oven:

BARDING Tie a thin layer of fat completely around the roast or chicken. Ask your butcher to do this for you, or use sheets of pork fatback or bacon slices and secure them with butcher's twine. As the roast cooks, the fat does the basting for you, protecting the meat while adding extra flavor. If you're watching your calories, discard the layer of crispy fat before serving (the fat doesn't travel deep into the roast). Instead of fat, you can also wrap the roast with a crust made from foods such as crushed potato chips, seasoned dried potato flakes, corn flakes, or ground dried mushrooms, which helps to seal in the juices.

LARDING Rendered and clarified pork fat is known as lard. Look for processed lard, as it is firmer and has a longer shelf life than the unprocessed variety. It has also been filtered, bleached, hydrogenated, or emulsified to give the lard a milder flavor. Southerners have used lard for centuries to make piecrusts flakier and more tender.

Inserting thin, long strips (lardons) of fat into a roast is called larding. Use a larding needle, which you can find in specialty food shops. One basic kind has a sharp, pointed tip and a hollow body. Insert a thin strip of fat or some bacon into the hollow and thread the fat through the meat. It's a quick way to ensure that a lean roast comes out of the oven tender, flavorful, and succulent. Some folks lard meat to add flavor, or instead of fat, thread slivers of fresh garlic in beef roasts, or fresh rosemary leaves in a rack of lamb.

BEEF UP THE FLAVOR WITH MIREPOIX

At one time, mirepoix was one of the best-kept secrets among French chefs. But word has finally gotten out. These three aromatic ingredients— onions, carrots, and celery—are placed in the bottom of a roasting pan before adding the roast—to make a soup, stock, stew, sauce, gravy, or marinade. It's the base-flavoring technique in many French kitchens.

To get the best flavor from mirepoix, here are a few tips:

- Pick the mirepoix ingredients based on the ingredients and flavoring in the main dish you're creating. Some are basic, such as the Cajun Trinity (see page 15), while others vary with the dish.
- For the best flavor, peel all vegetables before dicing them for a mirepoix (since items like onion skins, for example, can add undesired color). Though some chefs advocate only using peeled vegetables for a mirepoix— especially if they are being strained out and don't end up in the finished dish—others believe that peeling vegetables allows more flavor to travel into the dish.
- Cut pieces the same size to match the cooking time of the dish—the shorter the simmering and cooking time, the smaller and thinner the cut; and, conversely, the longer the cooking time, the larger the cut. This means: Cut the ingredients larger for pot roasts and stews; smaller for pan gravies and dishes that simmer up to 3 hours; and finer still for pan gravies and sauces that simmer less than 1 hour.
- When roasting, it's fine to spread the uncooked mirepoix on the bottom of the pan before adding the meat.
- To produce even more flavor, smother the mirepoix in beef stock or brown it in the roasting pan in the oven before adding the meat.

Here are a few mirepoix combinations that work well in oven dishes.

1. Standard French Mirepoix—onion (double the amount), carrot, and celery. Ideal for roasting beef. Use the mirepoix "as is," uncooked, or cook the onions in hot fat, then add the carrots and cook until it all turns brown. Add celery and cook just until it turns bright green. To intensify the flavor and color even more, stir in tomato paste and cook until the mixture turns a rich reddish brown before adding to the roasting pan.

2. *Battuto* (known as *Soffritto* after sautéing)—In addition to onion, carrot, and celery, Battuto also contains pancetta or fatback, green peppers, garlic,

Cooking Basics

6 DELICIOUS WAYS TO A GREAT STUFFED POTATO

Here's comfort food at its ever-loving best, all ready for supper right out of the oven. And what a fast, easy, delicious way to serve supper! An overstuffed baked potato that's brimming with cheese and other extras that turn it into a meal. All you need is a salad and you're done. That's the glory of cooking in the oven.

Here's how to cook 4 overstuffed 'taters. Take your pick from the extras below and get ready for supper, down-home style. Buy 4 large baking (russet) potatoes, each about 8 to 10 ounces. Scrub them, prick their skin a few times, rub them with a little oil, and pop them into a 400°F oven on the middle rack. Bake for 1 hour, or until soft and tender. Cut a ½-inch lengthwise slice off of each one, then scoop the potato flesh into a bowl. Warm ¾ cup milk and ½ stick butter until the butter is melted. Mash the potatoes by hand or with an electric mixer on medium, adding the milk mixture as you go. Fold in ¼ cup sour cream and season to your liking with salt and pepper. Stuff the potatoes back into their shells, mounding the top. Sprinkle each with 1 tablespoon grated Cheddar cheese and a little paprika. Put the potatoes in a shallow baking dish and bake for 15 minutes, or until piping hot. Serves 4 hungry folks!

Take your pick from these variations:

CHICKEN 'N' CHEESE—Fold in 1 cup chopped cooked chicken and ½ cup whipped cream cheese before stuffing.

BROCCOLI 'N' CHEESE—Cook one 10-ounce package chopped frozen broccoli according to package directions and drain well. Stuff potatoes as directed above. Spoon one-fourth of the broccoli on top and sprinkle each with ¼ cup shredded Cheddar and a little paprika.

CARAMELIZED ONIONS—Cut 2 medium yellow onions into thin slices. Sauté in a little butter until the onions turn golden. Drain. Stir into the potato mixture before stuffing.

HAM 'N' CHEESE—Fold in 1 cup chopped cooked ham and ¾ cup shredded Cheddar cheese before stuffing.

VEGETABLE MIX-UP—Prepare 1 package frozen broccoli, corn, and red peppers according to package directions and drain well. Stuff the potatoes as directed above. Spoon one-fourth of the vegetables on top of each potato and sprinkle with ¼ cup shredded Cheddar and a little paprika.

and parsley. It's perfect in Italian pasta bakes and other Italian-flavored soups and stews.

3. Cajun Trinity—onion, celery, and green pepper (instead of carrot). Use in Cajun dishes, such as a shrimp creole or seafood gumbo.

4. *Matignon* (eatable mirepoix)—In addition to onion, carrot, and celery, matignon also uses diced ham, mushrooms, herbs, and spices.

5. White Mirepoix—Substitute chopped leeks for half of the onion and substitute parsnips for half the carrots. Use in pale-colored stews such as Veal Blanquette, in cream-based dishes, or add to the pan before roasting chicken.

Take a few moments to browse through *Easy Oven Dishes* recipes and plan which ones to try right away. Here are some favorites:

Classic Lasagna   (page 18)

Mom's Mac & Cheese   (page 31)

Prime Rib with Traditional Yorkshire Pudding   (page 36)

Honey-Glazed Spareribs   (page 52)

Herb Butter Roasted Chicken   (page 62)

Oven-Fried Honey Chicken   (page 68)

Lemon Trout   (page 87)

Fisherman's Wharf Crab Bake   (page 89)

Baked Tomatoes with Herb Topping   (page 109)

Buttermilk Biscuits   (page 116)

Banana Apple Betty   (page 126)

Upside-Down Cake   (page 130)

Classic Lasagna, page 18

Prime Rib, page 36

Banana Apple Betty, page 126

Mom's Mac & Cheese, page 31

Casseroles & Pasta Bakes

Casseroles make the best comfort food! They're easy fixing, good eating, and often bring back wonderful memories. So get out your casserole dish and stir up a tuna noodle casserole. This one is similar to the classic you remember, except it's probably richer tasting, thanks to two cans of soup instead of one. Many of the casseroles are put together faster than ever, thanks to ham from the deli, frozen ravioli, spaghetti sauce from a jar, and preshredded cheese. So make a lasagna from only six ingredients, layer manicotti with three cheeses, and toss together Mom's Mac & Cheese in just 20 minutes. Then let your oven do the rest.

CLASSIC LASAGNA

Prep **45 MINUTES**   *Cook* **1 HOUR 15 MINUTES**

8	ounces lasagna noodles
1	pound ground beef (85% lean)
1	jar (30 ounces) pasta sauce
1	container (30 ounces) ricotta cheese
1½	cups shredded Parmesan cheese (6 ounces)
3	tablespoons finely chopped parsley
3	cups shredded mozzarella cheese (12 ounces)

This lasagna can be assembled, covered, and refrigerated up to 24 hours before baking. To bake, cover with foil and bake in a preheated 350°F oven for 50 minutes. Then uncover and bake 15 minutes longer.

LET'S BEGIN Preheat the oven to 350°F. Cook the lasagna noodles according to the package directions. Drain and place on a kitchen towel in one layer. Meanwhile, cook the beef in a large skillet over medium heat for 6 minutes, or until brown, breaking it up with a spoon. Drain off any fat and stir in the pasta sauce.

LAYER Combine the ricotta, ¾ cup of the Parmesan, and the parsley in a medium bowl and stir to mix well. Spoon ¾ cup of the sauce mixture into a 13 × 9-inch baking pan. Layer one-third of the noodles, half of the ricotta mixture, one-third of the remaining sauce mixture, and 1 cup of the mozzarella in the pan. Repeat the layers.

INTO THE OVEN Top with the remaining noodles, sauce mixture, and mozzarella. Sprinkle the top with the remaining Parmesan. Cover and bake for 50 minutes. Uncover and bake 15 minutes longer. Let stand for 10 minutes for easier serving.

Makes 12 servings

Per serving: 243 calories, 32g protein, 22g carbohydrates, 26g fat, 14g saturated fat, 89mg cholesterol, 813mg sodium

ITALIAN SAUSAGE & PASTA BAKE

Prep **20 MINUTES**   *Cook/Bake* **35 MINUTES**

8	ounces ziti or mostaccioli pasta
1	pound mild or hot Italian sausage
1	large onion, chopped
2	garlic cloves, minced
1	red bell pepper, cut into 1-inch squares
1	green bell pepper, cut into 1-inch squares
1	can (14½ ounces) diced tomatoes or Italian-style tomatoes
1	can (6 ounces) tomato paste
¼	cup chopped fresh basil or 2 teaspoons dried
2	cups Italian shredded cheese with garlic (8 ounces)

Just for fun, substitute mostaccioli pasta for the ziti. Translated, its name means "little moustaches," and they look just like them— 2-inch tubes that are usually ridged.

LET'S BEGIN Preheat the oven to 375°F. Cook the pasta according to the package directions. Drain and keep warm.

FLASH INTO THE PAN Meanwhile, cut the sausage into ½-inch pieces and discard the casings. Cook the sausage in a large skillet over medium heat for 5 minutes, or until it is browned on all sides. Pour off the drippings. Add the onion, garlic, and peppers and cook for 5 minutes or until the sausage is cooked through and the vegetables are crisp-tender.

INTO THE OVEN Add the tomatoes and tomato paste and stir to mix well. Stir in the pasta and the basil and transfer the mixture to a 13 × 9-inch baking dish. Cover and bake for 20 minutes. Uncover and sprinkle with the cheese and bake 5 minutes longer, or until the cheese melts.

Makes 6 servings

Per serving: 515 calories, 25g protein, 28g carbohydrates, 34g fat, 15g saturated fat, 86mg cholesterol, 832mg sodium

3-CHEESE MANICOTTI

Prep **20 MINUTES**   *Cook* **40 MINUTES**

1   package (8 ounces) manicotti shells

1   container (15 ounces) ricotta cheese

¾   cup shredded Parmesan cheese (3 ounces)

½   cup seasoned dry bread crumbs

¼   cup chopped fresh parsley

1   large egg

3   cups shredded mozzarella cheese (12 ounces)

1   jar (28 ounces) pasta sauce

Using already shredded cheese sure cuts down on the kitchen time. When the manicotti is removed from the oven, let it rest for a good 10 minutes, making it easier to serve.

LET'S BEGIN Preheat the oven to 350°F. Cook the manicotti shells according to the package directions. Drain and set aside. Combine the ricotta, ½ cup of the Parmesan, the bread crumbs, parsley, and egg and stir to mix well. Stir in 2 cups of the mozzarella.

LAYER Spread ½ cup of the pasta sauce onto the bottom of a 13 × 9-inch baking dish. Spoon ¼ cup of the cheese mixture into each manicotti shell and place in the baking dish. Repeat with the remaining cheese mixture and the manicotti shells.

BUBBLE & BAKE Pour the remaining pasta sauce over the manicotti and sprinkle with the remaining mozzarella and Parmesan. Bake for 30 minutes, or until the cheese is melted and the sauce is bubbly.

Makes 6 servings

Per serving: 511 calories, 33g protein, 38g carbohydrates, 26g fat, 15g saturated fat, 105mg cholesterol, 1,692mg sodium

SuperQuick
RAVIOLI BAKE

Prep **5 MINUTES**   *Cook* **21 MINUTES**

This casserole is great weeknight food. Why not bake a double batch and enjoy one for dinner one night and freeze the second one for another night?

1   package (12 ounces) frozen cheese ravioli

1½   pounds ground beef (85% lean)

½   cup chopped onion

Salt

Ground black pepper

1   can (26½ ounces) green pepper and mushroom spaghetti sauce

2   small zucchini, thinly sliced

1½   cups shredded mozzarella cheese (6 ounces)

LET'S BEGIN Preheat the oven to 400°F. Cook the ravioli according to the package directions. Drain and keep warm. Coat an 8 × 8-inch baking dish with cooking spray and set aside.

MAKE IT SAUCY Cook the beef and onion in a large skillet over medium heat for 6 minutes, or until brown, breaking it up with a spoon. Drain off any fat. Season to taste with the salt and pepper. Stir in the spaghetti sauce and zucchini.

LAYER & BAKE Place half of the ravioli in the prepared pan. Top with half of the sauce mixture, then with half of the cheese. Repeat the layering. Bake for 15 to 20 minutes, or until heated through.

Makes 6 servings
Per serving: 638 calories, 40g protein, 44g carbohydrates, 32g fat, 14g saturated fat, 142mg cholesterol, 1,092mg sodium

On the Menu

Take out your favorite red-checked tablecloth, open a bottle of Chianti, and set out some candles. You'll feel just like you're in an Italian trattoria.

Baked Clams Oreganata

Arugula and Radicchio Salad with Parmesan Shavings

Balsamic Vinaigrette

3-Cheese Manicotti

Chocolate Gelato or Ice Cream

Almond Biscotti

Espresso

ZESTY ZITI BAKE

Prep **15 MINUTES**   *Cook* **1 HOUR**

1   pound ziti or rigatoni

1   teaspoon vegetable oil

1   large onion, chopped

3   garlic cloves, minced

2   medium zucchini, diced

1   can (28 ounces) crushed tomatoes in puree

2   teaspoons dried Italian seasoning

¼   teaspoon each red-pepper flakes and salt

⅛   teaspoon ground black pepper

2   egg whites

1   container (15 ounces) part-skim ricotta cheese

⅔   cup shredded part-skim mozzarella cheese (3 ounces)

⅓   cup grated Parmesan cheese

This casserole tastes best if allowed to sit, covered loosely, for about 30 minutes. The flavors just seem to come together.

LET'S BEGIN Preheat the oven to 325°F. Prepare the pasta according to the package directions. Drain and transfer to a 3-quart casserole dish. Meanwhile, heat the oil in a large skillet over medium-low heat. Add the onion and garlic and cook for 5 minutes, or until softened. Add the zucchini, tomatoes, Italian seasoning, red-pepper flakes, salt, and pepper. Cover and cook, stirring occasionally, for 10 minutes, or until the vegetables are soft.

LAYER & BAKE Combine the egg whites and the ricotta in a medium bowl, stir to mix well, and spoon over the pasta. Top with the vegetable mixture and sprinkle with the mozzarella and Parmesan. Bake for 45 minutes, until the top is golden brown.

Makes 6 servings

Per serving: 500 calories, 27g protein, 73g carbohydrates, 11g fat, 6g saturated fat, 34mg cholesterol, 786mg sodium

Cooking Basics

EASY WAYS TO PREPARE PASTA FOR OVEN DISHES

A pasta casserole is the quintessential comfort food—homey, hearty, and delicious. Before you head to the kitchen, brush up on these basics:

• Always slightly undercook pasta. Since it gets a second cooking in the oven, it'll continue to absorb liquid and get more tender.

• Cover the top layer of pasta with sauce or cheese; otherwise the pasta will get dry and hard.

• To save on kitchen time, cook the pasta ahead and drain it well (very important!). Toss it with a bit of olive oil and refrigerate in a resealable plastic bag.

• If you have time to assemble everything, most pasta casseroles can be put together hours ahead and then refrigerated until they're ready to be baked.

• Most pasta casseroles need a good rest (at least 10 minutes) before being served. In fact, layered casseroles, such as lasagna, are even better if allowed to rest for about 30 minutes (cover it loosely to keep it hot).

BEEF NACHO CASSEROLE

Prep **10 MINUTES**   *Cook* **26 MINUTES**

1   pound ground beef (85% lean)

1   jar (12 ounces) thick and chunky salsa

1   cup frozen whole kernel corn

¾   cup mayonnaise

1   tablespoon chili powder

2   cups crushed tortilla chips

2   cups grated Monterey Jack cheese (8 ounces)

1   tomato, sliced

Everyone's favorite—nachos—gets even better when cooked into a hearty beef casserole. Use your favorite tortilla chips.

LET'S BEGIN Preheat the oven to 350°F. Cook the beef in a large skillet over medium heat for 6 minutes, or until brown, breaking it up with a spoon. Drain off any fat. Stir in the salsa, corn, mayonnaise, and chili powder.

LAYER IT Spread one-half of the meat mixture into an 8-inch square baking pan. Top with 1 cup of the chips and sprinkle the chips with 1 cup of the cheese. Repeat the layering with the remaining meat mixture, chips, and cheese.

INTO THE OVEN Bake for 20 minutes, or until heated through. Top with the tomato slices and serve immediately.

Makes 6 servings

Per serving: 660 calories, 26g protein, 22g carbohydrates, 52g fat, 16g saturated fat, 95mg cholesterol, 961mg sodium

Food Facts

THE CASSEROLE: TRULY A 1950s AMERICAN PHENOMENON

Most historians agree that the casserole can be traced far back in history as the French term of *cassole* (cassolette), which later became casserole.

At the beginning of the 18th century in England, a casserole was a rice dish, molded in the shape of a cooking pot and filled with a savory mixture, such as sweetbreads or chicken. By the late 19th century, a casserole was a dish of meat, vegetables, or stock that was cooked slowly in a closed pot in the oven. That definition remains today.

Several factors led to the popularity of casseroles in the 1950s. Early American cookbooks, including Fannie Farmer's and Marion Harland's, as well as women's magazines, depicted casserole cooking as a tried-and-true type of meal preparation. These first recipes often suggested a casserole as a way to use leftovers—a message that grew in importance during World Wars I and II. What better way to stretch meat and other ingredients than to combine them in a casserole? The Campbell Soup Company made it even easier: Just open a can of soup—voilà, sauce!

Cookware manufacturers also contributed to the evolution by introducing numerous attractive casseroles that easily traveled from oven to table. And the rise in brunches, church socials, buffets, and patio parties in suburbia meant that the portable, easy-to-serve casserole was here to stay.

MEDITERRANEAN-STYLE PIEROGIES

Prep **20 MINUTES**   *Cook* **20 MINUTES**

1   package (16.9 ounces) frozen potato and Cheddar pierogies

2   tablespoons olive oil

2   cups peeled, cubed eggplant

1   medium onion, chopped

2   teaspoons minced garlic

1   can (14½ ounces) tomatoes with basil and oregano

¼   cup sliced black olives

1   tablespoon balsamic vinegar

1   teaspoon dried thyme

¾   cup grated Parmesan cheese

You can use almost any variety of black olives here. If you prefer a subtle olive taste, stick with California black olives. But if you are an olive lover, choose kalamata, niçoise, or Gaeta olives and make a bolder statement.

LET'S BEGIN Preheat the oven to 350°F. Lightly grease a 2-quart baking dish and set aside. Cook the pierogies according to package directions, drain, and transfer to the prepared dish.

FLASH INTO THE PAN Meanwhile, heat the oil in a large skillet over medium heat. Add the eggplant, onion, and garlic and cook, stirring often, for 3 minutes, or until lightly browned. Stir in the tomatoes, olives, vinegar, and thyme and spoon the mixture over the pierogies. Toss gently to coat.

INTO THE OVEN Cover and bake for 10 minutes, or until heated through. Sprinkle with the cheese.

Makes 4 servings

Per serving: 420 calories, 16g protein, 51g carbohydrates, 17g fat, 6g saturated fat, 82mg cholesterol, 1,116mg sodium

HOBO CASSEROLE

Prep **15 MINUTES**   *Cook* **1 HOUR 22 MINUTES**

1	pound ground beef (85% lean)
¼	cup chopped onion
1	stalk celery, chopped
1	teaspoon salt
¼	teaspoon ground black pepper
1	can (10¾ ounces) condensed tomato soup, undiluted
¼	cup ketchup
2	teaspoons Worcestershire sauce
1	can (10¾ ounces) sliced potatoes, drained
1	package (10 ounces) frozen peas
1	package (10 ounces) frozen whole baby carrots

We love this casual casserole with ground beef, but you can also make it with ground pork or ground turkey. Serve it with an iceberg lettuce and tomato salad and end the meal with fudgy brownies.

LET'S BEGIN Preheat the oven to 350°F. Cook the beef, onion, and celery in a large skillet over medium heat for 6 minutes, or until the meat is brown, breaking it up with a spoon. Drain off any fat and stir in the salt and pepper.

MIX IT UP Combine the soup, ketchup, and Worcestershire sauce in a 3-quart casserole and stir to mix well. Add the beef mixture, the potatoes, peas, and carrots and stir to combine.

INTO THE OVEN Cover and bake for 1 hour and 15 minutes, or until hot and bubbly.

Makes 8 servings

Per serving: 237 calories, 14g protein, 22g carbohydrates, 10g fat, 4g saturated fat, 39mg cholesterol, 778mg sodium

CHEESY HAM & NOODLE CASSEROLE

Prep **10 MINUTES**   Cook **50 MINUTES**

8   ounces medium noodles

2   tablespoons butter or margarine

1   medium onion, chopped

½   cup chopped green bell pepper

1   can (10½ ounces) condensed cream of mushroom soup, undiluted

1   cup sour cream

2   cups shredded Swiss cheese (8 ounces)

2   cups cubed cooked ham (about ¾ pound)

Save on the prep work by buying ham at the deli counter and requesting that it be sliced about a half inch thick. Then stack the slices and cut them into cubes. Easy!

LET'S BEGIN Preheat the oven to 350° F. Cook the noodles according to the package directions. Drain and keep warm. Grease a 2-quart casserole dish and set aside.

FLASH INTO THE PAN Melt the butter in a medium saucepan over medium heat. Add the onion and pepper and cook, stirring often, for 5 minutes, or until softened. Remove the pan from the heat and stir in the soup and the sour cream.

LAYER & BAKE Place one-third of the noodles into the prepared pan. Top with one-third of the cheese, one-third of the ham, and half of the soup mixture. Repeat the layering, ending with final third of noodles, cheese, and ham. Bake for 35 to 40 minutes, or until heated through.

Makes 6 servings

Per serving: 513 calories, 27g protein, 38g carbohydrates, 29g fat, 15g saturated fat, 123mg cholesterol, 1,180mg sodium

---

Time Savers

DO-AHEAD TRICKS FOR OVEN DISHES

Nothing beats an oven for no-fuss cooking! We all enjoy knowing that dinner is safely minding itself in the oven while we take care of other things. But if speed is your need, here are some tricks that will make oven cooking as fast as it is convenient.

Precook vegetables, particularly root vegetables, for several minutes while the oven is preheating. Then add them, steaming hot, to the roast or oven dish.

Brown sausage, onions, and other vegetables before adding them to the stuffing. If the bird is going in the oven immediately, it is perfectly safe to fill it with warm stuffing. (It starts cooking faster!)

Sear roasts and chops in a heavy flameproof roasting pan or Dutch oven on the stove top and put them into the oven in the same hot pan. If you're adding liquid, bring it to a boil first.

Cover dense vegetable casseroles, such as scalloped potatoes, and bake until just tender or heated through. Then uncover, add toppings such as cheese or crumbs, and increase the heat to brown them.

CORNBREAD & BEEF CASSEROLE

Prep **10 MINUTES**   *Cook* **1 HOUR**

1	pound ground beef (90% lean)
1	can (15 ounces) cream-style corn
1	cup milk
2	large eggs, lightly beaten
¼	cup vegetable oil
1	cup yellow cornmeal
2	teaspoons baking soda
1	teaspoon salt
1	can (7 ounces) diced green chiles
2	cups shredded Cheddar cheese (8 ounces)
1	large onion, chopped

Choose lean ground beef for this dish: 90 percent or higher, especially since the fat is drained off. And use mild, sharp, or extra sharp Cheddar, whichever you prefer.

LET'S BEGIN Preheat the oven to 350°F. Lightly grease a 10-inch ovenproof skillet and set aside. Cook the beef in a large skillet over medium heat for 6 minutes, or until brown, breaking it up with a spoon. Drain off any fat. Set the beef aside.

MIX IT UP Combine the corn, milk, eggs, and oil in a large bowl and stir to mix well. Add the cornmeal, baking soda, and salt and stir until well combined.

LAYER & BAKE Pour half of the corn mixture into the prepared skillet. Top with the beef, chiles, 1½ cups of the cheese, and the onion. Pour the remaining cornmeal mixture over the top and spread to cover the filling. Top with the remaining cheese. Bake for 50 minutes, or until golden brown. Let the casserole stand for 5 minutes for easier serving.

Makes 8 servings

Per serving: 446 calories, 22g protein, 29g carbohydrates, 28g fat, 12g saturated fat, 125mg cholesterol, 1,074mg sodium

CLASSIC TUNA NOODLE CASSEROLE

Prep **15 MINUTES**   *Cook* **55 MINUTES**

2   cups medium egg noodles

1   can (6 ounces) solid white albacore tuna in oil, drained and flaked

1   cup fresh or frozen and thawed peas

1   large onion, chopped

1   can (10¾ ounces) cream of mushroom soup, undiluted

1   can (10¾ ounces) condensed cream of celery soup, undiluted

½   cup milk

½   teaspoon ground black pepper

4   ounces (1 sleeve) saltine crackers, crushed

1   cup grated Parmesan cheese

Tuna noodle casserole was developed by the Campbell Soup Company around 50 years ago, and its popularity has never waned. This rendition is even tastier than the original as it uses both cream of mushroom and cream of celery soup.

LET'S BEGIN Preheat the oven to 375°F. Cook the egg noodles according to the package directions. Drain the noodles and place in a large bowl. Coat a shallow 2-quart casserole dish with cooking spray and set aside.

MIX IT UP Add the tuna, peas, and onion to the noodles and stir to mix well. Whisk together the mushroom and celery soups, milk, and pepper in a medium bowl. Pour over the noodle mixture and stir to combine.

INTO THE OVEN Spread the mixture evenly into the prepared dish. Sprinkle the crushed saltines and the cheese over the top. Bake for 45 minutes, until heated through and the top is golden. Let cool slightly before serving.

Makes 4 servings

Per serving: 540 calories, 29g protein, 57g carbohydrates, 22g fat, 8g saturated fat, 59mg cholesterol, 1,935mg sodium

MOM'S MAC & CHEESE

Prep **20 MINUTES**   *Cook* **55 MINUTES**

1	pound elbow macaroni
4	cups shredded mild Cheddar cheese (1 pound)
4	cups shredded sharp Cheddar cheese (1 pound)
½	teaspoon salt
¼	teaspoon pepper
1	can (12 ounces) evaporated milk

This version of mac and cheese is definitely for cheese lovers! It is the cheesiest and the creamiest ever, so it makes a great side dish. Enjoy it with roasted chicken or broiled or grilled fish.

LET'S BEGIN Preheat the oven to 350°F. Cook the macaroni according to package directions. Drain and keep warm. Coat a 13 × 9-inch baking dish with cooking spray.

LAYER IT Arrange half of the macaroni in the prepared dish. Sprinkle with 2 cups of the mild Cheddar and 2 cups of the sharp Cheddar. Repeat the layering with the remaining macaroni, the salt, pepper, and the cheeses.

BUBBLE & BAKE Pour the milk evenly over the top. Bake for 45 minutes, or until golden brown and bubbly.

Makes 8 servings

Per serving: 719 calories, 38g protein, 49g carbohydrates, 41g fat, 24g saturated fat, 133mg cholesterol, 911mg sodium

Cook to Cook

WHAT ARE SOME TASTY WAYS TO VARY MAC & CHEESE?

"Though it seems almost impossible to get tired of plain macaroni and cheese, sometimes my family looks forward to one of my easy and tasty variations. I begin with a basic recipe that serves four, and I then use one of the following:

Macaroni and cheese *with mushrooms and bacon.* Cook 4 to 6 slices of bacon until crisp, then crumble them. Sauté about 6 ounces of white or cremini mushrooms until all of their liquid has evaporated. Stir the bacon and mushrooms into the macaroni and cheese mixture and bake as your recipe directs.

Macaroni and cheese *with sun-dried tomatoes and olives.* Prepare the macaroni and cheese as the recipe directs. Stir in about 6 thinly sliced sun-dried tomatoes and ½ cup of chopped pitted olives. Bake as your recipe directs.

Macaroni and cheese *with blue cheese and walnuts.* Prepare the macaroni and cheese as directed, but use blue cheese and fontina cheese instead. After the mixture is spooned into the prepared baking dish, sprinkle with about ½ cup of toasted chopped walnuts.

Tex-Mex macaroni and cheese. Prepare the macaroni and cheese as directed in the recipe, but use shredded Mexican blend cheese and stir in a small can of drained chopped green chiles and 1 package of taco seasoning mix."

Stuffed Pork Chops, page 50

Mostly Meats

Here's the collection of recipes you'd expect to find in this book—old-fashioned pot roast, stuffed pork chops, baked ham, and meat loaf. But what may be surprising is that most of these dishes are ready to go into the oven in less than 20 minutes. Our beef brisket bakes in its own oven bag, which guarantees it will come out juicier and yummier than you ever remembered. And the short ribs braise inside the oven where they stay nice and moist, without any watching from you. We've also tucked in a way to get two suppers out of one prime rib recipe and tips on how to slice preparation time out of meat loaf and other oven dishes. It's all part of quick cooking to give you fabulous down-home dinners, without the fuss.

Smokin' Calypso Brisket

Prep **10 MINUTES**   *Cook* **1 HOUR 45 MINUTES**

1	tablespoon flour
1	large foil cooking bag
1	boneless beef brisket, trimmed (2 to 4 pounds)
1½	cups barbecue sauce
⅓	cup hot-pepper sauce
4	teaspoons dried jerk seasoning

When opening a very hot, steam-filled foil bag, be sure to wear oven mitts and open the bag facing away from you. Take advantage of any leftovers and make some tasty sandwiches. Pile thinly sliced brisket on split hamburger buns and serve with deli coleslaw.

LET'S BEGIN Preheat the oven to 450°F. Sprinkle the flour into a large foil cooking bag and place the beef in the bag. Combine the barbecue sauce, hot-pepper sauce, and jerk seasoning in a small bowl and stir to mix well. Pour 1 cup of the mixture over the beef and seal the foil bag with tight double folds.

INTO THE OVEN Place the bag in a large baking dish and bake for 1¾ to 2½ hours, or until the beef is fork tender. Carefully open the bag, allowing the steam to escape.

SAUCE IT Place the remaining sauce in a small saucepan and cook over medium heat for 3 minutes, or until hot. Serve the sauce with the sliced brisket.

Makes 6 servings

Per serving: 472 calories, 29g protein, 9g carbohydrates, 35g fat, 14g saturated fat, 122mg cholesterol, 869mg sodium

WINTER BBQ BEEF SHORT RIBS

Prep **15 MINUTES**   *Cook* **1 HOUR 50 MINUTES**

4	pounds well-trimmed beef chuck short ribs, cut into 3 × 2-inch pieces
1	can (8 ounces) tomato sauce
¾	cup tomato juice
¼	cup minced onion
3	tablespoons cider vinegar
2	tablespoons Worcestershire sauce
¼	teaspoon ground cinnamon

Dash ground cloves

Dash ground black pepper

This dish is sure to keep away the winter doldrums. These ribs are some of the most delicious ones around! Serve with thick wedges of cornbread, carrot slaw, and creamy mashed potatoes.

LET'S BEGIN Adjust the broiler rack so that it is 3 to 4 inches from the heat. Preheat the broiler. Place the ribs on a rack in a broiler pan and broil for 20 minutes, or until well browned, turning occasionally.

INTO THE OVEN Preheat the oven to 350°F. Transfer the ribs to an ovenproof Dutch oven. Add all the remaining ingredients and bring to a boil over medium-high heat. Cover and bake for 1½ to 2 hours, or until the ribs are fork-tender.

SERVE IT UP Remove the ribs to a serving platter, skim the fat from the sauce, and serve the sauce with the ribs.

Makes 6 servings

Per serving: 240 calories, 24g protein, 6g carbohydrates, 13g fat, 5g saturated fat, 73mg cholesterol, 417mg sodium

PRIME RIB WITH TRADITIONAL YORKSHIRE PUDDING

Prep **15 MINUTES** Cook **1 HOUR 30 MINUTES**

1	rolled beef prime rib roast (4 to 5 pounds)
6	garlic cloves, each cut lengthwise into thirds
4	carrots, cut into 1-inch pieces
2	medium onions, each cut into 8 wedges
½	cup chopped fresh parsley
2	bay leaves
1	cup water
2	teaspoons chopped fresh thyme or 1 teaspoon dried
½	teaspoon salt
1	teaspoon ground black pepper
	Traditional Yorkshire Pudding (see recipe)

This impressive—yet easy—dish is the perfect centerpiece for a holiday dinner. Yorkshire pudding is simply a popover-type mixture that is flavored with butter or the pan drippings. Absolutely delicious!

LET'S BEGIN Preheat the oven to 450°F. Place the roast in a large roasting pan and cut 18 slits into the meat just large enough for the garlic slices. Insert a slice of garlic into each slit.

SEASON & SPICE Place the carrots, onions, parsley, and bay leaves around the roast and pour the water over the vegetables. Stir together the thyme, salt, and pepper in a small bowl and sprinkle the mixture over the roast.

INTO THE OVEN Bake for 30 minutes. Reduce the oven temperature to 325°F and bake 1 hour to 1 hour and 15 minutes longer, or until a meat thermometer reaches 130°F for medium-rare or to a desired degree of doneness. Cover the roast loosely with foil to keep warm while you make the Traditional Yorkshire Pudding.

Makes 10 servings

Per serving: 250 calories, 26g protein, 5g carbohydrates, 13g fat, 6g saturated fat, 80mg cholesterol, 190mg sodium

TRADITIONAL YORKSHIRE PUDDING

Preheat the oven to 400°F. Place ⅓ cup butter or beef drippings in a 13 × 9-inch baking pan and place in the oven to heat for about 5 minutes. Meanwhile, combine 1¾ cups all-purpose flour, 1 cup milk, 1 cup cold water, 4 large eggs, 1½ teaspoons seasoned salt, and ¼ teaspoon ground black pepper in a large bowl and beat at low speed with an electric mixer for 1 to 2 minutes, until smooth. Pour the batter into the hot pan and bake for 35 to 45 minutes, or until the edges are dark golden brown and the center is set. Serve immediately.

Makes 8 servings

Per serving: 226 calories, 7g protein, 22g carbohydrates, 12g fat, 5g saturated fat, 130mg cholesterol, 391mg sodium

Corned Beef & Cabbage

Prep **20 MINUTES**   *Cook* **3 HOURS**

1   corned beef brisket (3 to 3½ pounds)

1   cup apple cider or apple juice

2   teaspoons whole black peppercorns

3   bay leaves

1   pound small whole white onions

4   medium potatoes, peeled and cut into quarters

1   medium rutabaga, peeled and cut into 2-inch chunks (4 cups)

1   small head cabbage, cut into 8 wedges

Mustard Sauce (see recipe)

Celebrate St. Paddy's Day the classic way—with corned beef and cabbage. A quick and tasty mustard sauce made with only three ingredients makes this rendition special.

LET'S BEGIN Preheat the oven to 325°F. Place the brisket in a large roasting pan.

SEASON & SPICE Add the cider, peppercorns, bay leaves, and the seasoning packet from the brisket package. Cover and bake for 2 hours. Remove the pan from the oven and add the onions, potatoes, rutabaga, and cabbage.

INTO THE OVEN Cover and bake 1 to 1½ hours longer, or until the brisket is fork tender and the vegetables are done. Serve with Mustard Sauce.

Mustard Sauce

Pour 1 cup whipping cream into a medium bowl and beat at high speed with an electric mixer until stiff peaks form. Gently stir in ½ cup horseradish mustard and 2 tablespoons balsamic or red wine vinegar. (If you can't find horseradish mustard, use ¼ cup country-style Dijon mustard and ¼ cup prepared horseradish.) Serve with the brisket and vegetables.

Makes 10 servings

Per serving: 482 calories, 27g protein, 25g carbohydrates, 31g fat, 13g saturated fat, 109mg cholesterol, 1,857mg sodium

BEEF AND BROCCOLI AU GRATIN

Prep **15 MINUTES**   *Cook* **25 MINUTES**

1	package (6 ounces) broccoli rice au gratin mix
1	pound lean ground beef (85% lean)
1	cup chopped green bell pepper
1	cup chopped onion
1	can (8 ounces) tomato sauce
1	tablespoon dried Italian seasoning
1/3	cup shredded mozzarella cheese

A tasty broccoli-rice mix makes this dish ready for the oven in 15 minutes. So it's perfect for weeknights when time is short.

LET'S BEGIN Preheat the oven to 450°F. Cook the rice mix according to the package directions. Coat a 2-quart baking dish with cooking spray and set aside.

FLASH INTO THE PAN Meanwhile, cook the beef, bell pepper, and onion in a large skillet over medium heat for 6 minutes, or until the beef is brown, breaking it up with a spoon. Stir in the tomato sauce and the Italian seasoning and bring to a boil. Reduce the heat and simmer for 5 to 7 minutes.

INTO THE OVEN Transfer the rice to the prepared dish. Spoon the beef mixture over the rice and sprinkle with the cheese. Bake for 10 minutes, or until the mixture is heated through and the cheese melts.

Makes 8 servings

Per serving: 243 calories, 14g protein, 20g carbohydrates, 12g fat, 5g saturated fat, 45mg cholesterol, 512mg sodium

Food Facts

THE CORNED IN CORNED BEEF

Did you know that the term *corned* comes from the English use of the word corn, meaning a small particle, such as salt or grain? During the 1800s in New England, much time was devoted to preserving food in preparation for the cold winters ahead. A New England boiled dinner often included preserved corned beef and a variety of vegetables that were slowly cooked together in a large pot that hung from a crane or hook in front of the fire.

Traditionally, in those early colonies, corned beef was put on to cook right after Sunday breakfast on Sunday, then served at noon after church services. Any leftovers reappeared as hash on Monday. The platter always included beets as one of the vegetables, thus the corned beef hash turned out red. Some say the red color is how it got the name Red Flannel Hash, because of the likeness in color to red flannel underwear.

In England, corned beef is served in a classic salad with lettuce leaves, tomato quarters, slices of beetroot, and salad cream (a rich dressing for salads made from cream, quite different from our mayonnaise). Corned beef hash is also a favorite throughout Great Britain.

In Ireland, corned beef is held in even higher regard. For centuries, it has been a traditional dish to serve at Christmas, Easter, and always on St. Patrick's Day with cabbage.

SUNDAY SUPPER MEAT LOAF WITH ROASTED VEGETABLES

Prep **15 MINUTES**   *Cook* **50 MINUTES**

1½   pounds lean ground beef (85% lean)

¾   cup oats

¾   cup minced chopped onion

1   large egg, lightly beaten

½   cup chili sauce or ketchup + extra for basting (optional)

1   tablespoon Worcestershire sauce

2   garlic cloves, minced

1   teaspoon dried thyme leaves

¾   teaspoon ground black pepper

½   teaspoon salt (optional)

Roasted Vegetables (see recipe)

Adding oats to meat loaf is such a smart idea. Not only are oats healthful, but they also make the loaf nice and moist. Mixing the meat mixture with a light hand ensures that the meat loaf will be very tender. Use an instant-read thermometer to tell when the loaf is done. It should read 160°F.

LET'S BEGIN Preheat the oven to 350°F. Combine all the ingredients except the Roasted Vegetables in a large bowl and mix lightly but thoroughly.

SHAPE & BAKE Shape the mixture into an 8 × 4-inch loaf on the rack of a broiler pan. Bake for 50 to 55 minutes or until the meat loaf is done.

SAUCE IT Brush with additional chili sauce during the last 10 minutes of baking, if you wish. Serve with the Roasted Vegetables.

Makes 6 servings
Per serving: 470 calories, 26g protein, 44g carbohydrates, 21g fat, 7g saturated fat, 105mg cholesterol, 440mg sodium

ROASTED VEGETABLES

Combine 1½ pounds medium red potatoes, quartered; 1 pound carrots, cut diagonally into ¾-inch pieces; 1 small yellow onion, cut lengthwise into ½-inch wedges; 2 tablespoons olive oil; 2 garlic cloves, minced; ¾ teaspoon dried thyme leaves; ½ teaspoon salt; and ¼ teaspoon black pepper in a large bowl. Toss to combine. Transfer to a large baking pan and bake in a preheated 350°F oven for 50 to 55 minutes, or until tender, stirring once.

SuperQuick
ROAST BEEF CHEDDAR POCKETS

Prep **15 MINUTES**   *Cook* **13 MINUTES**

1   package (16 to 17 ounces) refrigerated fully cooked boneless beef pot roast with gravy

1   package (8 ounces) refrigerated crescent rolls

1   cup shredded sharp Cheddar cheese (4 ounces)

⅓   cup minced sweet onion (optional)

¼   cup sour cream

Fresh chives (optional)

This is the kind of food that is perfect for a birthday or Saturday lunch at home with the kids. Put together the pockets and set them aside in the refrigerator until you are ready to bake them.

LET'S BEGIN Preheat the oven to 375°F. Remove the pot roast from the package and reserve the gravy for another use. Cut the roast into fine shreds. Unroll the crescent dough onto an ungreased baking sheet. Separate into 4 rectangles and press the diagonal seams to seal. Pull the sides of the rectangles slightly to enlarge them.

FILL & FOLD Combine the beef, ¾ cup of the cheese, and the onion in a large bowl and stir to mix well. Divide the beef mixture into 4 portions and press each one between your palms to compact it. Place one portion of the beef mixture in the center of each piece of dough. Fold the long sides of each rectangle over the filling and press at the top to seal. Press the ends to seal.

INTO THE OVEN Sprinkle the pockets evenly with the remaining cheese and bake for 13 to 16 minutes or until golden brown. Serve with the sour cream and garnish with the chives, if you wish.

Makes 4 servings

Per serving: 436 calories, 23g protein, 25g carbohydrates, 28g fat, 13g saturated fat, 69mg cholesterol, 847mg sodium

Time Savers

A GREAT WAY TO SPEED UP MEAT LOAF

Traditionally, a meat loaf made from 2 pounds of ground beef is shaped in a 9 × 5 × 3-inch loaf pan, resembling a loaf of bread. It usually requires about 1¼ hours to bake in a moderate oven (350°F). It's done when an instant-read thermometer inserted into the center of the loaf reads 160°F.

To bake meat loaf in less time, put the meat mixture into a 13 × 9-inch baking dish and shape into a larger, thinner loaf (12 × 8 inches). Spoon chili sauce (right out of the bottle) on top. Bake at 350°F until the internal temperature reaches 160°F. This thinner loaf will cook in less time, about 45 to 50 minutes. And the best part: Each person gets a long slice with more chili sauce on top.

BEEF-STUFFED PEPPERS

Prep **15 MINUTES**   *Cook* **1 HOUR**

4	medium green, red, or yellow bell peppers
1	pound lean ground beef (85% lean)
1	large onion, chopped
¼	cup long-grain white rice
4	tablespoons ketchup
1	teaspoon dried oregano
½	teaspoon salt
¼	teaspoon ground black pepper
1	can (14½ ounces) Italian-style stewed tomatoes

It's fun to use a mix of bell peppers; they come in such happy colors. The easiest way to cut off the pepper tops is with a serrated knife. Just shake the peppers to remove any stray seeds. And don't forget to rinse the peppers well.

LET'S BEGIN Preheat the oven to 350°F. Cut the tops off the bell peppers and remove the seeds.

STUFF 'EM Place the beef, onion, rice, 3 tablespoons of the ketchup, ½ teaspoon of the oregano, the salt, and black pepper in a large bowl. Stir the mixture lightly to combine and spoon it into the peppers. Stand the peppers upright in an 8 × 8-inch baking dish.

MAKE IT SAUCY Combine the tomatoes and the remaining ketchup and oregano in a small bowl and stir to mix well. Pour over the peppers. Cover and bake for 1 to 1½ hours, or until the beef is cooked through and the peppers are tender.

Makes 4 servings

Per serving: 390 calories, 24g protein, 28g carbohydrates, 20g fat, 8g saturated fat, 78mg cholesterol, 763mg sodium

---

Microwave in Minutes

CUT THE OVEN TIME WHEN MAKING STUFFED PEPPERS

Let your microwave help you cut the baking time for stuffed peppers. Precook them in the microwave until just tender before stuffing them. The effect is the same as blanching them in a big pot of water—but it's faster and easier. Here's how:

• Select 4 sweet bell peppers of uniform size and shape for even cooking.

• Slice the top off each from the stem end, about ¾ inch down. Remove and discard the seeds and membranes.

• To make sure the peppers stand up straight during cooking, cut a very thin slice off the base of each. Be careful not to cut into the hollow cavity.

• Stand the peppers in a microwaveable casserole and add 1 tablespoon of water to the casserole. Cover with plastic wrap, leaving a corner open 1 to 2 inches.

• Microwave on High for about 2 minutes, or until hot. Let the casserole rest, covered, on the counter for about 2 minutes, or until the peppers are just barely tender.

• Stuff and bake them as directed—but watch the baking time. They'll be ready to serve in much less time than if you began with uncooked peppers.

HONEY-GLAZED RACK OF LAMB

Prep **15 MINUTES + MARINATING**   *Cook* **26 MINUTES**

¼   cup olive oil

3   tablespoons minced shallots

2   garlic cloves, minced

½   cup lemon juice

¼   cup honey

1   tablespoon chopped fresh thyme

Salt

Ground black pepper

2   2-pound racks of lamb

Fresh thyme is great in this recipe, but if you prefer to use dried, here is the basic substitution rule: Use about one-third of the amount of a dried herb for the fresh. So, here you should use approximately 1 teaspoon of dried thyme.

LET'S BEGIN Heat the oil in a medium saucepan over medium heat. Add the shallots and cook for 5 minutes, or until softened. Stir in the garlic and cook for 1 minute. Remove from the heat and stir in the lemon juice, honey, thyme, and salt and pepper to taste. Let the honey sauce cool.

MARINATE Place the lamb in a large shallow dish. Pour ½ cup of the honey sauce over the lamb and turn to coat evenly. Cover and refrigerate 1 hour. Set the remaining honey sauce aside. Preheat the oven to 425°F.

INTO THE OVEN Place the lamb, meat side up, in a foil-lined baking pan. Bake for 20 to 25 minutes, until a meat thermometer registers 130°F to 135°F for medium rare, or to the desired degree of doneness. Let the lamb stand, loosely covered with foil, for 10 minutes before carving. Drizzle each serving with the remaining honey sauce.

Makes 4 servings

Per serving: 930 calories, 59g protein, 22g carbohydrates, 66g fat, 30g saturated fat, 210mg cholesterol, 200mg sodium

APRICOT-GLAZED HAM

Prep **10 MINUTES**   *Cook* **1 HOUR 30 MINUTES**

1	**fully cooked whole boneless ham (5 pounds)**
²⁄₃	**cup apricot nectar**
2	**tablespoons lemon juice**
¹⁄₃	**cup firmly packed brown sugar**
1	**tablespoon cornstarch**
¹⁄₂	**teaspoon ground nutmeg**
¹⁄₄	**teaspoon ground cloves**

This ham is only baked to 140°F because it is purchased already fully cooked, so all you have to do is heat it through. The apricot nectar mixture beautifully glazes the ham and adds great flavor.

LET'S BEGIN Preheat the oven to 325°F. Place the ham on a rack in a shallow roasting pan.

INTO THE OVEN Bake, uncovered, for 1¼ hours, or until a meat thermometer registers 140°F.

GLAZE IT Meanwhile, combine the remaining ingredients in a small saucepan. Cook over medium heat, stirring constantly, for 2 minutes, until thickened and bubbly. Brush the ham with the glaze and bake 15 to 20 minutes longer, brushing occasionally with the glaze.

Makes 20 servings

Per serving: 208 calories, 25g protein, 6g carbohydrates, 9g fat, 3g saturated fat, 64mg cholesterol, 1,572mg sodium

On the Menu

---❖---

Let this delicious pork supper transport you to the islands before you take the first bite!

---❖---

Honeydew & Cantaloupe & Toasted Coconut

Caribbean Roast Pork

Shredded Cabbage & Carrot Stir-Fry

Broiled Fresh Pineapple Rings

Lemon Sorbet & Almond Cookies

CARIBBEAN ROAST PORK

Prep **10 MINUTES**   Cook **1 HOUR**

It's very safe to cook pork to 155°F because when it rests, the temperature will rise 5° to 10°F. Round out the meal with pineapple rice and oven-roasted carrots.

2	teaspoons olive oil
1	teaspoon ground nutmeg
1	teaspoon ground cinnamon
1	tablespoon ground black pepper
1	pork loin roast (3 pounds)

LET'S BEGIN Preheat the oven to 350°F. Combine the first 4 ingredients in a small bowl and stir to mix well.

SEASON IT Place the roast in a shallow roasting pan and brush with the olive oil mixture.

INTO THE OVEN Bake for 1 to 1½ hours, or until a thermometer inserted into the center registers 155°F. Let the roast stand for 10 minutes before slicing.

Makes 6 servings

Per serving: 240 calories, 30g protein, 1g carbohydrates, 12g fat, 4g saturated fat, 85mg cholesterol, 60mg sodium

PEPPERED PORK POT ROAST

Prep **20 MINUTES**   *Cook* **1 HOUR 45 MINUTES**

2   teaspoons olive oil

2   pounds boneless pork shoulder roast or pork sirloin roast

1   large onion, chopped

3   celery stalks, thinly sliced

1   can (15 ounces) chunky Italian tomato sauce

1   can (14½ ounces) beef broth + additional beef broth, if needed

1   tablespoon lemon juice

1   teaspoon ground black pepper

½   teaspoon cayenne pepper

4   medium Yukon Gold potatoes, quartered

4   medium parsnips, peeled, halved lengthwise, and cut into 2-inch pieces

1   medium rutabaga, peeled, quartered, and cut into ¼-inch slices

3   tablespoons cornstarch

¼   cup cold water

2   tablespoons minced fresh parsley

Hot cooked orzo pasta

This is the perfect dish for wintry evenings when comfort food is needed. Pork shoulder and sirloin roasts are especially moist and flavorful and are perfect for pairing with hearty root vegetables.

LET'S BEGIN Preheat the oven to 350°F. Heat the olive oil in a nonstick skillet over medium-high heat. Add the pork, and cook, turning occasionally, for 8 minutes, until browned on all sides. Remove the pork and set aside. Add the onion and celery to the skillet and cook, stirring often, for 5 minutes, or until tender. Drain off any fat. Stir in the tomato sauce, 1 can of the broth, and the lemon juice. Transfer the onion mixture to a shallow 4-quart casserole dish. Sprinkle the black and cayenne peppers over the pork and place it in the casserole dish. Cover, transfer to the oven, and bake for 30 minutes.

INTO THE OVEN Remove the casserole dish from the oven and transfer the pork to a plate. Place the potatoes, parsnips, and rutabaga in the casserole dish and then set the pork on top of the vegetables. Cover and bake 1 hour longer, or until the roast and vegetables are tender.

MAKE IT SAUCY Transfer the pork and the vegetables to a large serving platter and cover with foil to keep warm. Transfer the pan juices to a 4-cup measuring cup and skim off any fat. Add the additional broth or water, if needed, to measure 3½ cups. Transfer the mixture to a medium saucepan and place over medium heat. Stir together the cornstarch and ¼ cup water in a small bowl and add to the saucepan. Cook, stirring constantly, for 1 to 2 minutes, or until the mixture comes to a boil and thickens. Stir in the parsley and transfer the sauce to a serving bowl. Serve with cooked orzo.

Makes 8 servings
Per serving: 447 calories, 27g protein, 55g carbohydrates, 13g fat, 4g saturated fat, 66mg cholesterol, 518mg sodium

SPICY CRANBERRY PORK CHOPS

Prep **10 MINUTES**   *Cook* **25 MINUTES**

1   can (16 ounces) whole berry cranberry sauce

½   cup raisins

½   cup peeled, diced apple

¼   cup + 2 tablespoons sugar

¼   cup + 2 tablespoons vinegar

⅛   teaspoon ground allspice

⅛   teaspoon ground ginger

⅛   teaspoon ground cinnamon

Dash of ground cloves

4   boneless pork loin chops (4 ounces each)

Cranberry sauce just loves to be mixed with warm spices such as allspice, ginger, cinnamon, and cloves. You don't need much, as they are quite potent.

LET'S BEGIN Preheat the oven to 350°F. Combine all of the ingredients except the pork in a medium saucepan and cook over medium heat, stirring occasionally, for 10 minutes, or until the apples are tender and the sauce has thickened slightly. Set aside and keep warm.

INTO THE OVEN Meanwhile, place the chops in a single layer in a baking pan and bake for 15 minutes.

MAKE IT SAUCY Remove the pan from the oven and top each chop with ¼ cup of the sauce. Bake 10 minutes longer, or until the chops are done. Serve the chops with the remaining sauce.

Makes 4 servings

Per serving: 524 calories, 25g protein, 84g carbohydrates, 11g fat, 4g saturated fat, 54mg cholesterol, 113mg sodium

STUFFED PORK CHOPS

Prep **15 MINUTES + COOLING**   *Cook* **1 HOUR 20 MINUTES**

1   teaspoon butter or margarine

2   medium onions, diced

2   stalks celery, diced

2   cups chicken broth

4   slices day-old bread, cut into ¼-inch cubes

¼   cup chopped fresh parsley

½   teaspoon dried basil

Salt

Ground black pepper

6   (2-inch thick) boneless pork chops (6 ounces each)

Extra-thick boneless pork chops are fabulous for stuffing. And this dish is great company food that is also easy to prepare. The easiest way to cut a pocket is with a boning knife. Be sure to insert the knife right in the middle of the chop and to use a gentle sawing motion.

LET'S BEGIN Melt the butter in a large nonstick skillet over medium heat. Add the onions and celery and cook, stirring often, for 5 minutes, or until softened. Add the broth and cook, uncovered, for 15 minutes, or until the liquid is reduced by half. Stir in the bread cubes, parsley, basil, and salt and pepper to taste. Remove from the heat and let cool.

STUFF IT Preheat the oven to 325°F. Cut a horizontal slit in each pork chop to form a pocket. Stuff one-fourth of the bread mixture into each chop and close the pockets with toothpicks.

INTO THE OVEN Place in a large baking pan and bake for 1 hour, or until cooked through. Remove toothpicks before serving.

Makes 6 servings

Per serving: 332 calories, 40g protein, 13g carbohydrates, 12g fat, 4g saturated fat, 96mg cholesterol, 583mg sodium

HONEY-GLAZED SPARERIBS

Prep **15 MINUTES**   *Cook* **1 ½ HOURS**

4   pounds lean pork
      spareribs

Salt

Ground black pepper

½   cup honey

¼   cup lemon juice

2   teaspoons grated lemon
      zest

2   teaspoons grated fresh
      ginger

1   garlic clove, minced

1   teaspoon dried rosemary,
      crushed

½   teaspoon red-pepper
      flakes

½   teaspoon ground sage

Honey does two fabulous things to these spareribs. It contributes just the right amount of sweetness, and it also coats the ribs with a caramelized glaze. Get ready to hear lots of raves. Just double the recipe if you want enough for seconds and leftovers the next day.

LET'S BEGIN Preheat the oven to 450°F. Place the ribs in a large pot or a deep skillet and add water to cover. Place over medium heat and bring to boil. Cook for 4 minutes. Remove ribs from pot.

SEASON & SPICE Sprinkle both sides of the ribs with salt and pepper to taste and place on a rack in a roasting pan. Cover loosely with foil and bake for 15 minutes.

INTO THE OVEN Meanwhile, combine all of the remaining ingredients in a small bowl and stir to mix well. Reduce the oven temperature to 350°F. Remove the pan from the oven and brush the ribs with the honey mixture. Bake 1 hour longer, brushing with the honey mixture every 15 minutes, until the ribs are tender.

Makes 4 servings
Per serving: 941 calories, 48g protein, 37g carbohydrates, 66g fat, 25g saturated fat, 218mg cholesterol, 217mg sodium

SAUSAGE & RICE BAKE

Prep **15 MINUTES**   *Cook* **1 HOUR**

1	pound bulk pork sausage
1	medium onion, chopped
1	cup long-grain white rice
1	cup chopped celery
½	(4.2-ounce) box chicken noodle soup mix
2	cups boiling water
1	cup finely shredded Cheddar cheese (4 ounces)

If you are shredding the cheese yourself, it's easiest if you pop it into the freezer for a little bit, just to firm it, not freeze it.

LET'S BEGIN Heat the oven to 350°F. Cook the sausage and onion in a large skillet over medium heat for 6 minutes, or until the sausage is brown, breaking it up with a spoon. Drain off any fat. Meanwhile, combine the rice, celery, soup mix, and water in a 2½-quart casserole and stir to mix well. Spoon the sausage mixture evenly over the rice mixture.

BAKE & SERVE Cover and bake for 50 minutes, or until the rice is tender. Remove the casserole from the oven, uncover, and stir to mix well. Sprinkle the cheese over the top and bake 5 minutes longer, or until the cheese melts.

Makes 6 servings

Per serving: 436 calories, 19g protein, 35g carbohydrates, 24g fat, 10g saturated fat, 70mg cholesterol, 1,183mg sodium

BEEF CASSEROLE ITALIANO

Prep **10 MINUTES**   *Cook* **40 MINUTES**

1½	cups (6 ounces) penne pasta
1	pound ground beef (85% lean)
1	can (14½ ounces) diced tomatoes with green pepper and onion
1	can (14½ ounces) peas and carrots, drained
1	can (10¾ ounces) cream of mushroom soup, undiluted
1½	cups shredded mozzarella cheese (6 ounces)

Begin the meal with an antipasto platter and breadsticks. Pick up a creamy ricotta cheesecake for dessert.

LET'S BEGIN Preheat the oven to 375°F. Cook the pasta according to the package directions. Drain and keep warm. Coat an 11 × 7-inch baking dish with cooking spray and set aside. Meanwhile, cook the beef in a large skillet over medium heat for 6 minutes, or until brown. Drain off any fat. Add the pasta, vegetables, and mushroom soup and stir until well combined.

INTO THE OVEN Transfer the mixture to the prepared pan, cover, and bake for 20 minutes. Remove the pan from the oven, uncover, sprinkle with the cheese, and bake 5 minutes longer, or until the cheese melts.

Makes 6 servings

Per serving: 453 calories, 27g protein, 33g carbohydrates, 24g fat, 10g saturated fat, 75mg cholesterol, 924mg sodium

CRISPY MANDARIN RIBLETS

Prep **10 MINUTES + MARINATING**　　*Cook* **45 MINUTES**

4	pounds pork spareribs, cut crosswise into thirds
¼	cup light soy sauce
2	tablespoons dry sherry
1	garlic clove, crushed

Mandarin Peach Sauce (see recipe)

Cutting spareribs crosswise in thirds makes them so easy to eat (ask your butcher to cut them). These make fabulous appetizers with the sauce served alongside for dipping. Don't forget to set out bowls for the bones and lots of pretty napkins.

LET'S BEGIN Cut the spareribs into individual ribs and place in a steamer basket or on a steamer rack. Set the basket or rack over a pan of boiling water, cover the pan, and steam for 30 minutes.

MARINATE Meanwhile, combine the soy sauce, sherry, and garlic in a large bowl. Add the ribs and stir to coat. Let the ribs stand to marinate for 1 hour, stirring frequently.

INTO THE OVEN Preheat the oven to 425°F. Remove the ribs from the marinade and place them, meaty side up, on the rack of a broiler pan. Discard the marinade. Bake for 15 minutes, or until browned and crispy. Serve with warm Mandarin Peach Sauce.

MANDARIN PEACH SAUCE

Drain a 15-ounce can of sliced peaches and process them in a blender until smooth. Place the peaches in a small saucepan. Stir together 2 tablespoons teriyaki sauce and 1 tablespoon cornstarch and stir into the peaches. Add 1 tablespoon sugar, ¼ teaspoon fennel seed, ¼ teaspoon ground black pepper, and ⅛ teaspoon ground cloves to the peach mixture. Bring to a boil over medium heat, stirring constantly, for 2 minutes, until the sauce mixture comes to a boil and thickens. Makes 1 cup.

Makes 6 servings

Per serving: 564 calories, 36g protein, 19g carbohydrates, 36g fat, 13g saturated fat, 143mg cholesterol, 950mg sodium

---

Cooking Basics

HOW TO BUY THE RIGHT RIBS

What's the best way to season and cook a slab of ribs? It often depends on where you live. Regardless of how you like them, the first step is to be sure you buy the right cut.

• Spareribs are the most reasonably priced type of ribs on the market. Select a slab that weighs no more than 3 pounds and is meaty between the ribs.

• For easier serving, ask your butcher to cut them into 1- or 2-rib intervals or to cut the spareribs into riblets.

• Supermarkets often package half slabs weighing about 1½ pounds. Check carefully: One end of a sparerib slab is always meatier.

• Ribs labeled "St. Louis style" have the breastbone removed, making it easy to cut between the ribs. They have more meat than spareribs.

• Baby back ribs are actually cut from the loin. They have smaller bones and more meat than spareribs. They often come cut into 2 to 4 rib servings.

• Country-style ribs contain bones of various sizes and shapes and a meaty chunk of pork loin.

• Buy about 1 pound of spareribs, ¾ pound of baby back ribs, or ½ pound of country-style ribs per serving. You might want to buy a little extra, just in case. Chances are, folks will want seconds!

COUNTRY QUICHE

Prep **15 MINUTES**   *Cook* **35 MINUTES**

1   tablespoon butter or
     margarine

½   cup chopped celery

½   cup chopped green bell
     pepper

1   medium onion, chopped

1   frozen deep-dish piecrust

2   ounces diced lean ham
     or turkey ham (½ cup)

2   ounces shredded
     reduced-fat Cheddar
     cheese (½ cup)

6   large eggs

1   cup skim milk

½   teaspoon paprika

½   teaspoon salt (optional)

Onion slices separated into
     rings (optional)

Scallion curls (optional)

Quiche has been adored throughout France for many years. It's simply a custard mixture flavored with a delicious variety of savory ingredients and baked in a pastry shell.

LET'S BEGIN Preheat the oven to 375°F. Heat the butter over medium heat in a medium skillet. Add the celery, pepper, and onion and cook, stirring occasionally, for 5 minutes, until the vegetables soften. Transfer the vegetables to the crust and top with the ham and cheese.

WHISK & POUR Combine the eggs, milk, paprika, and salt, if you wish, in a large bowl. Whisk until well blended and pour into the crust.

INTO THE OVEN Bake for 30 to 40 minutes, or until a knife inserted near the center comes out clean. Let the quiche stand for 5 minutes for easier serving. Garnish with the onion rings and scallion curls, if you wish.

Makes 6 servings

Per serving: 226 calories, 13g protein, 15g carbohydrates, 17g fat, 5g saturated fat, 229mg cholesterol, 450mg sodium

NEVER-FAIL CHEESE SOUFFLÉ

Prep **10 MINUTES + STANDING**   *Cook* **1 HOUR**

1	loaf (8 ounces) French or Italian bread, preferably day old
½	pound ham, cubed
1	package (14 ounces) frozen baby broccoli florets
2	cups shredded Cheddar cheese (8 ounces)
6	large eggs
2½	cups milk
2	tablespoons butter or margarine, melted
2	tablespoons Dijon mustard
1	teaspoon salt
¼	teaspoon ground black pepper

Here's a way to serve a spectacular soufflé for company, even if you've never made one before. Don't worry—it's guaranteed to come out high and light. Frozen broccoli florets really cut down on your kitchen time without sacrificing any flavor. Be sure to use the broccoli while it's still frozen. Tip: You can assemble this casserole, cover, and refrigerate it up to 24 hours before baking.

LET'S BEGIN Cut the bread into ¾-inch cubes. Coat a 13 × 9-inch baking dish with cooking spray and arrange half of the bread in the dish.

LAYER IT Top with half of the ham, half of the broccoli, and half of the cheese. Repeat the layering with the remaining bread, ham, broccoli, and cheese. Press the top down lightly. (The dish will be very full.)

INTO THE OVEN Combine the remaining ingredients in a large bowl and whisk to mix well. Pour over the cheese layer in the dish and let it stand for 15 minutes. Preheat the oven to 350°F. Bake for 1 hour, or until the top is golden brown.

Makes 8 servings

Per serving: 375 calories, 24g protein, 22g carbohydrates, 21g fat, 11g saturated fat, 217mg cholesterol, 1,253mg sodium

BACON CHEDDAR PUFFS

Prep **15 MINUTES** *Cook* **35 MINUTES**

8	slices bacon
1	cup milk
4	tablespoons butter or margarine
1	cup all-purpose flour
4	large eggs
4	ounces shredded sharp Cheddar cheese (1 cup)
½	teaspoon onion salt or powder
¼	teaspoon garlic salt
¼	teaspoon ground black pepper

The dough that is used for these savory puffs is known as pâte au choux (pronounced "pot ah shoo") in French. In fact, it is the same dough used to make éclairs and profiteroles (ice cream puffs). The key is to be sure to dump in the flour all at once and to stir it very vigorously. We recommend using your favorite wooden spoon. Puffs may be baked, cooled completely, and frozen for up to 1 month. Reheat the frozen puffs in a preheated 350°F oven for 8 to 10 minutes, or until heated through.

LET'S BEGIN Preheat the oven to 350°F. Cook the bacon until it is crisp. Drain on paper towels, crumble, and set aside. Coat two baking sheets with cooking spray and set aside.

FLASH IN THE PAN Combine the milk and butter in a medium saucepan. Cook over medium heat, stirring frequently until the butter is melted and the mixture is simmering. Add the flour and stir until the mixture forms a ball. Remove from the heat. Stir in the eggs, one at a time, until the mixture is smooth. Add the bacon, cheese, onion salt, garlic salt, and pepper and stir to mix well.

INTO THE OVEN Drop by heaping teaspoons onto the prepared pans and bake for 25 minutes, or until puffed and golden brown. Serve warm or at room temperature.

Makes 3 dozen puffs

Per puff: 48 calories, 2g protein, 3g carbohydrates, 3g fat, 2g saturated fat, 14mg cholesterol, 105mg sodium

MINI PINEAPPLE BACON GALETTES

Prep **20 MINUTES**   *Cook* **25 MINUTES**

6   slices bacon

1   can (8 ounces) crushed
    pineapple, drained

1   tablespoon maple syrup

1   teaspoon all-purpose
    flour

1   package (15 ounces)
    refrigerated piecrusts

1   large egg

1   tablespoon water

A galette is a round of pastry dough that is covered with a sweet or savory filling. The dough edges are folded up and over only part of the filling, then it is baked. Here, refrigerated piecrusts make fast work of these tasty galettes.

LET'S BEGIN Preheat the oven to 400°F. Cook the bacon, drain on paper towels, cool, and crumble. Coat two baking sheets with cooking spray and set aside. Combine the bacon, pineapple, maple syrup, and flour in a small bowl and set aside.

FILL & BAKE Cut ten 3¾-inch circles from the piecrusts, using a biscuit cutter. Place on the prepared baking sheets. Spread 1 tablespoon of the pineapple filling over each crust. Fold the edges up over the filling, overlapping the dough to make pleats. Beat the egg and water together in a small bowl. Brush the edges of the crusts with the egg mixture. Bake for 16 to 18 minutes, or until the crusts are golden.

Makes 10 servings
Per serving: 316 calories, 4g protein, 25g carbohydrates, 22g fat, 8g saturated fat, 45mg cholesterol, 355mg sodium

Chicken Cordon Bleu, page 69

Chicken du Jour

There's nothing like watching the smiles on the faces of family members and friends when you bring out a Sunday roasted chicken. The one in this chapter is first coated with butter, which guarantees it will come out of the oven golden, crispy, and delicious every time—with little watching from you. But don't stop there. Thumb through these recipes and discover many more yummy ways that chicken can go in and out of the oven. Pecan-coat it and oven-fry it as they do in the South. Or toss it into a potpie or a quiche, let it bake on its own inside foil packets, or smother it with tomatoes and Parmesan as they do in Italy. Then pick out a delicious chicken dish to slide into the oven for dinner tonight.

Herb Butter Roasted Chicken

Prep **10 minutes**   *Cook* **2 hours**

1	chicken (4 to 5 pounds)
¼	cup unsalted butter, softened
2	tablespoons chopped fresh parsley
2	tablespoons chopped fresh rosemary or 1 teaspoon dried
1	teaspoon minced garlic
1	teaspoon salt
¼	teaspoon ground black pepper

Pear, plum, and/or apricot slices (optional)

Rubbing a whole chicken with a flavored butter does two things: It makes the skin crispy and brown and also flavors the chicken. Make a double or triple batch of the butter, roll it into a narrow log (about 1½ inches in diameter), wrap it tightly in foil, and freeze it for up to two months. Then cut off thick slices of the frozen butter and use it to top fish, vegetables, or potatoes.

LET'S BEGIN Preheat the oven to 350°F. Tuck the chicken wings under the bird and tie the legs together using kitchen twine.

RUB IT ON Combine the butter, parsley, rosemary, garlic, salt, and pepper in a small bowl and stir to mix well. Rub the mixture onto the chicken and place it breast side up on a rack in a roasting pan.

INTO THE OVEN Bake for 2 to 2½ hours, basting occasionally, or until the chicken is cooked through and a meat thermometer inserted into the inner thigh reaches 180°F. Add the pear, plum, and/or apricot slices to the roasting pan 10 minutes before the end of the baking time, if you wish, and serve with the roasted chicken.

Makes 6 servings

Per serving: 460 calories, 42g protein, 0g carbohydrates, 31g fat, 12g saturated fat, 155mg cholesterol, 520mg sodium

Chicken with Roasted Vegetables

Double the butter and seasoning ingredients and rub half of the mixture onto the chicken. Place 6 red potatoes, cut in half; 6 carrots, cut in half crosswise; and 3 medium onions, cut into quarters into the pan with the chicken. Spoon the remaining butter and seasoning mixture evenly over the vegetables. Bake as directed in the recipe above, basting the chicken and vegetables occasionally during baking.

SuperQuick

CRISPY LEMON CHICKEN

Prep **10 MINUTES**   *Cook* **20 MINUTES**

4	boneless, skinless chicken breast halves (about 1¼ pounds)
1	large lemon
⅓	cup reduced-fat mayonnaise
¼	cup grated Parmesan cheese
½	teaspoon dried oregano
2	tablespoons dry bread crumbs

This tasty chicken makes great sandwiches. Double the mayonnaise mixture and spread it on the bread for even more great flavor.

LET'S BEGIN Preheat the oven to 400°F. Blot the chicken pieces dry with paper towels. Grate the zest from the lemon and squeeze the juice from half of the lemon and mix together with the mayonnaise, Parmesan, and oregano.

SEASON 'EM Coat the chicken pieces with the lemon juice mixture and sprinkle with the bread crumbs.

INTO THE OVEN Place in a single layer in a baking pan and bake for 20 to 30 minutes, or until chicken is done.

> *Makes 4 servings*
>
> *Per serving: 360 calories, 57g protein, 7g carbohydrates, 11g fat, 3g saturated fat, 148mg cholesterol, 400mg sodium*

SOUTHERN PECAN CRUSTED CHICKEN

Prep **15 MINUTES**   *Cook* **50 MINUTES**

4	tablespoons butter or margarine, melted
1	can (5 ounces) evaporated milk
1	cup biscuit mix
½	cup finely chopped pecans
1	teaspoon paprika
1	teaspoon salt
½	teaspoon dried poultry seasoning
3	pounds cut-up chicken pieces

What a delicious idea—to combine finely chopped pecans with biscuit mix and use it to coat chicken for oven frying.

LET'S BEGIN Preheat the oven to 400°F. Coat the bottom of a large roasting pan with the butter and set aside. Pour the milk into a shallow dish. Mix together the remaining ingredients except chicken in a large, shallow dish.

DIP & COAT Dip each piece of chicken into the milk, then coat with the pecan mixture. Place the chicken skin side down in the roasting pan.

INTO THE OVEN Bake for 30 minutes. Remove the pan from the oven and turn the chicken pieces over. Bake 20 minutes longer, or until the chicken is cooked through.

> *Makes 4 servings*
>
> *Per serving: 765 calories, 40g protein, 26g carbohydrates, 55g fat, 17g saturated fat, 160mg cholesterol, 1,215mg sodium*

ROASTED CHICKEN WITH WINTER VEGETABLE STUFFING

Prep **20 MINUTES**   *Cook* **2 HOURS**

¼ teaspoon salt

¼ teaspoon ground black pepper

1 whole roasting chicken (5 pounds)

1 tablespoon butter or margarine

¼ teaspoon each ground cinnamon, cumin, and coriander

½ cup chicken broth

¾ cup dry sherry

1 tablespoon all-purpose flour

Winter Vegetable Stuffing (see recipe)

Roasting a whole chicken on a rack allows the air to circulate all around, ensuring the bird browns on the bottom.

LET'S BEGIN Preheat the oven to 400°F. Sprinkle the salt and pepper inside the cavity of the chicken. Melt the butter in a small saucepan over low heat. Stir in the cinnamon, cumin, and coriander. Brush the spice mixture over the chicken. Tuck the wings under the bird and tie the legs together using kitchen twine. Set the chicken on a rack in a roasting pan and add the chicken broth to the pan. Bake for 30 minutes. Reduce the oven temperature to 350°F. (If you are making the Winter Vegetable Stuffing to serve with the chicen, put it in the oven now.) Bake the chicken 1¼ hours longer, or until a meat thermometer inserted in the thigh reaches 180°F. Add several tablespoons of water during roasting if necessary.

MAKE IT SAUCY Remove the chicken to a serving platter and cover it loosely with foil to keep it warm. Skim the fat off the juices left in the roasting pan and place the pan over medium heat. Stir in the sherry and scrape off any browned bits of chicken stuck to the pan. Stir in the flour, bring to a boil, and cook for 1 minute to thicken. Serve with gravy and stuffing.

WINTER VEGETABLE STUFFING

Cook 1 medium diced onion in 1 tablespoon butter in a large skillet over medium heat until softened. Stir in ¼ teaspoon each ground cinnamon, cumin, and coriander and cook for 1 minute. Stir in 8 ounces diced fresh mushrooms, 1 cup coarsely grated parsnips, and 1 cup coarsely grated carrots. Cook for 6 minutes, or until the vegetables are tender. Stir in 1 cup toasted bread crumbs, ½ cup finely chopped toasted hazelnuts, ½ cup chicken broth, and ⅛ teaspoon each salt and ground black pepper. Bake in a 1½-quart baking dish at 350°F for 1¼ hours.

Makes 6 servings

Per serving: 565 calories, 30g protein, 27 carbohydrates, 34g fat, 9g saturated fat, 110mg cholesterol, 580mg sodium

DILL CHICKEN IN FOIL

Prep **15 MINUTES**   *Cook* **35 MINUTES**

8   skinless chicken thighs (about 2 pounds)

1   teaspoon salt

½   teaspoon ground black pepper

½   cup butter or margarine, melted

2   tablespoons lemon juice

½   teaspoon dried dill weed

4   tablespoons sliced scallions

1   cup thinly sliced carrots

8   slices Swiss cheese (1 ounce each)

Dried dill weed is a very convenient ingredient. But if you happen to have fresh dill on hand, snip 1 or 2 tablespoons and use it instead.

LET'S BEGIN Preheat the oven to 400°F. Sprinkle the chicken thighs with salt and pepper. Combine the butter, lemon juice, and dill weed in a small bowl and stir to mix well.

FOLD 'EM UP Cut four 12 × 18-inch squares of heavy duty foil and coat each with cooking spray. Drizzle 2 teaspoons of the butter mixture in the center of each sheet of foil and top with 2 chicken thighs. Top evenly with the scallions and carrots and drizzle with the remaining butter mixture. Top with the cheese slices. Bring up the foil sides and double fold the top and ends to seal the packet, leaving room for heat to circulate inside.

INTO THE OVEN Place the packets on a cookie sheet. Bake for 35 minutes, or until the chicken is cooked through.

Makes 4 servings

Per serving: 579 calories, 40g protein, 4g carbohydrates, 42g fat, 22g saturated fat, 220mg cholesterol, 1,786mg sodium

Cooking Basics

THE SECRET TO FOIL PACKET COOKING

Cook boneless chicken breasts inside foil packets in the oven—they'll go to the table moist, juicy, and done to perfection. Best of all, you can make them in the morning and refrigerate them until dinnertime.

To make individual packets:

• Place a boneless chicken breast half on the center of a piece of foil and top with the other ingredients.

• Bring up the foil sides and double fold it, leaving room for heat to circulate.

• Place the packets on a cookie sheet and bake for 30 to 35 minutes in a 400°F oven.

Tasty chicken combos:

• Chicken Dijon: Combine Dijon mustard and mayonnaise. Spread over the chicken and top with thinly sliced mushrooms and sweet onions.

• Primavera Chicken: Add asparagus, scallions, and snow peas, all sliced thinly on the diagonal. Top with a squeeze of lemon juice, salt, and a pat of butter.

• Chicken Italiano: Add shredded zucchini and chopped tomato. Season with salt, pepper, fresh oregano, and Parmesan cheese. Drizzle with olive oil.

• Southern Chicken: Add slices of canned sweet potatoes, top with a pineapple slice, sprinkle with brown sugar and cinnamon, and top with a pat of butter.

SuperQuick
BAKED CHICKEN WITH MANDARIN SAUCE

Prep **5 MINUTES** *Cook* **25 MINUTES**

4	boneless, skinless chicken breast halves (about 1¼ pounds)
1	can (5.3 ounces) evaporated milk
1	cup Italian-seasoned dry bread crumbs
1	cup orange juice
1	tablespoon cornstarch
½	teaspoon dried basil, crushed

Salt

Ground black pepper

1	can (11 ounces) mandarin oranges, drained

Chicken has a natural affinity for the taste of citrus, especially the fresh taste of mandarin oranges. Serve on fettucini.

LET'S BEGIN Preheat the oven to 425°F. Cut the chicken pieces in half crosswise. Place the milk in a shallow bowl and place the bread crumbs in another shallow bowl.

COAT & BAKE Dip the chicken in the milk and then dip in the bread crumbs to coat well. Bake on a rack in a roasting pan for 25 to 28 minutes, or until the chicken is cooked through.

MAKE IT SAUCY Meanwhile, combine the orange juice, cornstarch, and basil in a small saucepan and stir until the cornstarch dissolves. Cook the mixture over medium heat, stirring constantly, for 2 to 3 minutes, or until the mixture comes to a boil and thickens. Season to taste with the salt and pepper and stir in the oranges. Serve with the chicken.

Makes 4 servings

Per serving: 416 calories, 43g protein, 40g carbohydrates, 9g fat, 3g saturated fat, 108mg cholesterol, 562mg sodium

---

Food Facts

THE SOUTH'S LOVE AFFAIR WITH FRIED CHICKEN

We know that the English settlers brought chickens with them to the New World. The Scottish immigrants were the ones who loved their chicken fried. They likely taught the cooks on Southern plantations this fast, delicious way of cooking. The plantation workers loved to feast on fried chicken and grits on Sunday mornings. Even today, plantation breakfasts almost always feature a huge platter of Southern fried chicken, along with plenty of white, creamy country gravy (especially in Maryland), with hot biscuits to soak it all up.

Just how the chicken is seasoned, dipped, floured, or battered depends on where you live, the regional and family traditions, and who's working the stove that day. Some shake the chicken pieces only in seasoned flour, others dip it in a light fritter batter, while still others dip it in eggs, roll it in crushed cracker crumbs, and then bake it.

Even the cooking fat varies—from lard, butter, oil, or bacon fat to a combination of these. Most grab the family's black cast-iron skillet for frying—real Southern cooks wouldn't have it any other way.

Through time, one thing has remained constant: Southerners love their fried chicken hot, crispy, and well seasoned. Even today, you'll find all different ways to make fried chicken, and it'll always be on the menu down South.

OVEN-FRIED HONEY CHICKEN

Prep **10 MINUTES**   *Cook* **30 MINUTES**

¼   cup honey

2   tablespoons balsamic or
    red wine vinegar

1½   cups dry bread crumbs

1   tablespoon olive oil

6   boneless, skinless
    chicken breast halves
    (about 2 pounds)

Enjoy all of the tempting crunch of fried chicken with moist and tender chicken to boot. For easy cleanup, line the baking pan with foil.

LET'S BEGIN Preheat the oven to 375°F. Combine the honey and vinegar in a medium bowl and stir to mix well. Place the bread crumbs in a shallow dish. Line a large baking pan with foil and coat it with the oil.

DIP & COAT Dip each chicken breast into the honey mixture, then dredge in the bread crumbs.

INTO THE OVEN Place in the pan and bake for 30 minutes, or until the chicken is cooked through.

Makes 6 servings

Per serving: 335 calories, 39g protein, 31g carbohydrates, 6g fat, 1g saturated fat, 88mg cholesterol, 297mg sodium

CHICKEN CORDON BLEU

Prep **20 MINUTES** *Cook* **30 MINUTES**

4   boneless, skinless
    chicken breast halves
    (about 1 ¼ pounds)

1   tablespoon Dijon
    mustard

½   teaspoon dried thyme

2   slices reduced-fat Swiss
    cheese, cut into halves
    (1 ounce each)

4   thin slices ham
    (4 ounces)

¼   cup seasoned bread
    crumbs

1   tablespoon shredded
    Parmesan cheese

4   teaspoons reduced-fat
    margarine, melted

Chicken or veal cooked with prosciutto, or other ham, and Swiss cheese is called Cordon Bleu. Be sure to pound the chicken thoroughly so it is easy to roll up. Use a rolling pin or meat pounder.

LET'S BEGIN Preheat the oven to 400°F. Place each chicken breast between 2 pieces of plastic wrap and pound to ¼-inch thickness. Spread the mustard down the center of each chicken breast and sprinkle evenly with the thyme. Top each with a half slice of Swiss cheese and a slice of ham. Roll up each chicken breast and secure with toothpicks.

BRUSH & COAT Mix the bread crumbs and the Parmesan. Brush the chicken with the margarine and coat with the crumb mixture.

INTO THE OVEN Place the chicken in an 8 × 8-inch baking pan and bake for 10 minutes. Reduce the heat to 350°F and bake 20 minutes longer, or until the chicken is cooked through. Remove the toothpicks before serving.

Makes 4 servings

Per serving: 275 calories, 39g protein, 7g carbohydrates, 10g fat, 3g saturated fat, 89mg cholesterol, 790mg sodium

SuperQuick
CHICKEN PARMESAN

Prep **5 MINUTES**   *Cook* **25 MINUTES**

4   boneless, skinless
     chicken breast halves
     (about 1¼ pounds)

2   cans (14½ ounces each)
     diced Italian-style
     tomatoes with basil,
     garlic, and oregano

2   tablespoons cornstarch

¼   teaspoon hot-pepper
     sauce (optional)

⅓   cup grated Parmesan
     cheese

Flavorful Italian-style diced tomatoes are a great convenience food. All the garlic, basil, and oregano you need has already been added.

LET'S BEGIN Preheat the oven to 425°F. Pound chicken between 2 sheets of plastic wrap to flatten slightly.

INTO THE OVEN Place the chicken in a single layer in a baking dish, cover, and bake for 20 minutes. Uncover the dish and carefully drain off the liquid.

MAKE IT SAUCY Meanwhile, combine the tomatoes, cornstarch, and hot-pepper sauce, if desired, in a medium saucepan and stir to dissolve the cornstarch. Cook over medium heat, stirring constantly, for 5 minutes, or until the mixture comes to a boil and thickens. Pour the tomato sauce over the chicken and sprinkle the cheese over the top. Bake, uncovered, for 5 minutes, or until the sauce is bubbly and the cheese melts.

Makes 4 servings

Per serving: 385 calories, 60g protein, 22g carbohydrates, 5g fat, 2g saturated fat, 143mg cholesterol, 1,315mg sodium

---

Cook to Cook

WHAT ARE SOME FUN FOODS TO STUFF A CHICKEN WITH?

“I have heard chefs say that the ultimate test of their skills comes in roasting a perfect chicken. It is the stuffing, however, that gives roast chicken its identity—a personality all its own.

My favorite country classic is to sauté sliced Granny Smith apples, onions, and sprigs of fresh thyme in butter. Toss with cornbread cubes and a little broth.

For a fun Roman holiday, gently lift the bird's breast skin and stuff prepared pesto sauce under it. Add fresh basil leaves, chopped roasted peppers, olive oil, and garlic to Italian bread cubes for the interior stuffing.

If you prefer a taste of buffalo, sauté celery and carrots in oil, then toss with bread cubes and blue cheese dressing for

the stuffing. Brush the chicken with a mixture of butter and hot sauce.

I call this Carolina combo, prepare your favorite seasoned rice mix or pilaf recipe using a little less water than usual. Stir in toasted pecans and spoon into the chicken while hot. The chicken will cook quicker and you have a side dish inside. ”

CREOLE CHICKEN

Prep **15 MINUTES**   Cook **50 MINUTES**

The lemon slices serve two special purposes in this dish. They prevent the chicken coated with Creole spices from sticking to the roasting pan. Plus, as the chicken cooks, the lemons get nice and caramelized, adding even more flavor to this New Orleans dish.

1   lemon, peeled and sliced

6   skinless chicken breast halves, bone-in (about 3 pounds)

1½   tablespoons dried Creole seasoning

Salt

Ground black pepper

2   heads garlic, separated into cloves and pressed

1   cup chicken broth

⅔   cup dry white wine

1   tablespoon all-purpose flour

LET'S BEGIN Preheat the oven to 350°F. Arrange the lemon slices in a large roasting pan. Coat the chicken with the Creole seasoning, salt and pepper to taste, and the garlic. Place the chicken on top of the lemons.

MAKE IT SAUCY Combine the chicken broth, wine, and flour in a small bowl and stir to mix well. Pour into the roasting pan.

INTO THE OVEN Cover and bake for 50 to 60 minutes, or until the chicken is cooked through and the juices run clear. Serve the chicken with the sauce.

Makes 6 servings

Per serving: 294 calories, 56g protein, 4g carbohydrates, 3g fat, 1g saturated fat, 137mg cholesterol, 783mg sodium

On the Menu

In the Big Easy, where life is slow and sweet, Creole chicken is often on the menu. Dust off your wicker furniture and enjoy this Bourbon Street Supper on your back porch.

Shrimp with Rémoulade Sauce

Creole Chicken

Steamed White Rice

Sautéed Okra 'n' Tomatoes with Onions

Hot Cornbread Sticks

Peppered Butter

Vanilla Ice Cream with Toasted Pecans & Caramel Sauce

Chicory Coffee

CRISPY HERB-TOPPED CHICKEN

Prep **10 MINUTES**   *Cook* **30 MINUTES**

8   boneless, skinless chicken breast halves (about 2½ pounds)

2   cups shredded Swiss cheese (8 ounces)

1   can (10¾ ounces) cream of chicken soup, undiluted

¼   cup dry white wine (or milk)

1   tablespoon hot-pepper sauce

2   cups seasoned bread crumbs

⅓   cup melted butter

3   tablespoons slivered almonds

This dish is so tasty with Swiss cheese. Or, try other favorite good-melting cheese instead, including Gruyère, fontina, or Cheddar.

LET'S BEGIN Preheat the oven to 350°F. Place the chicken in a single layer in a large casserole dish. Sprinkle evenly with the cheese.

LAYER IT Combine the soup, wine, and hot-pepper sauce in a small bowl and stir to mix well. Spoon the mixture evenly over the chicken, spreading to cover completely. Top the chicken with the crumbs, drizzle with the butter, and sprinkle with the almonds.

INTO THE OVEN Bake for 30 to 35 minutes, or until the chicken is cooked through and the crumbs are lightly browned.

Makes 8 servings

Per serving: 612 calories, 68g protein, 27g carbohydrates, 24g fat, 11g saturated fat, 187mg cholesterol, 1,354mg sodium

VEGETABLE, CHICKEN & RICE CASSEROLE

Prep **15 MINUTES**   *Cook* **45 MINUTES**

1   can (10¾ ounces) cream of mushroom soup

1   cup milk

½   teaspoon garlic powder

1½   teaspoons salt

¼   teaspoon ground pepper

¾   cup long-grain white rice

1   large onion, chopped

1   package (16 ounces) frozen cauliflower, carrots, and snow peas blend

1   cup shredded Cheddar cheese (8 ounces)

4   boneless, skinless chicken breast halves

A colorful blend of frozen vegetables enlivens this comforting one-dish dinner recipe. Use mild, sharp, or extra-sharp cheese.

LET'S BEGIN Preheat the oven to 350°F. Mix the first 5 ingredients in a large bowl. Add the rice, onion, vegetable blend, and cheese and stir to combine.

INTO THE OVEN Coat a 9 × 13-inch baking dish with cooking spray and transfer the soup mixture to the dish. Top with the chicken, cover, and bake for 45 minutes, or until the rice and chicken are done.

Makes 4 servings

Per serving: 670 calories, 70g protein, 47g carbohydrates, 20g fat, 10g saturated fat, 173mg cholesterol, 1,904mg sodium

SuperQuick
PINEAPPLE CHICKEN PACKETS

Prep **15 MINUTES**   *Cook* **15 MINUTES**

1   cup coarsely shredded carrots

1   can (8 ounces) pineapple slices, drained

2   boneless, skinless chicken breast halves, cut in half lengthwise (about 5 ounces each)

½   teaspoon dried tarragon, crumbled

½   teaspoon grated lemon zest

1   teaspoon lemon juice

1   scallion, thinly sliced

Food steamed in foil (or parchment paper) packets makes cleanup a breeze—no pots or pans to wash! You can also count on the food to be very flavorful and juicy.

LET'S BEGIN Preheat the oven to 450°F. Tear off two 12 × 18-inch sheets of heavy-duty foil. Place half of the carrots in the center of each sheet. Top evenly with the pineapple, chicken, tarragon, lemon zest and juice, and scallion.

FOLD 'EM UP Bring up the foil sides and double fold the top and ends to seal the packets, leaving room for heat circulation inside.

INTO THE OVEN Place the packets on a cookie sheet and bake for 15 minutes, or until the chicken is cooked through. Let the packets stand for 5 minutes before opening.

Makes 2 servings

Per serving: 363 calories, 55g protein, 19g carbohydrates, 6g fat, 2g saturated fat, 148mg cholesterol, 173mg sodium

CURRIED CHICKEN POTPIE

Prep **20 MINUTES**   *Cook* **35 MINUTES**

1   cup chicken broth

¼   cup all-purpose flour

2   teaspoons curry powder

½   teaspoon salt

1   tablespoon vegetable oil

1¼   pounds boneless, skinless chicken breast halves, cut into ¾-inch pieces

1   medium onion, chopped

1   cup sliced carrots

1   Golden Delicious apple, peeled, cored, and cut into ½-inch pieces

½   cup frozen peas

½   cup light cream or unsweetened coconut milk

½   (15-ounce) package refrigerated piecrusts

Is there anyone who doesn't love potpie? Probably not. Here the chicken broth is whisked with the flour, ensuring that there will not be any lumps in the flavorful curry sauce.

LET'S BEGIN Preheat the oven to 425°F. Whisk the first 4 ingredients in a medium bowl and set aside. Heat the oil in a large skillet over medium-high heat. Add the chicken, onion, and carrots and cook, stirring constantly, for 5 minutes, or until the chicken is cooked through.

MAKE IT SAUCY Add the broth mixture to the skillet and bring to a boil. Stir in the apple pieces. Reduce the heat to medium and cook, stirring constantly, for 2 minutes, or until the sauce is thickened. Remove the skillet from the heat and stir in the peas and the cream. Spoon the mixture into a 9-inch deep-dish pie plate.

INTO THE OVEN Place the piecrust on top of the chicken and vegetables. Crimp or flute the edges around the rim of the pie plate to seal it tightly. Cut several small slits in the crust to allow the steam to escape. Place the pie plate on a cookie sheet and bake for 20 to 25 minutes, or until the top is golden.

Makes 6 servings

Per serving: 374 calories, 21g protein, 32g carbohydrates, 18g fat, 8g saturated fat, 67mg cholesterol, 573mg sodium

---

Time Savers

6 TRICKS TO HURRY UP POTPIES

Want to enjoy a potpie but don't want to spend hours making it? Here are some neat tricks to put a fabulous one together super-fast:

- Forget about using a double crust. A top crust is enough.
- Use refrigerated piecrust or biscuits for the topping, or leftover mashed potatoes.
- Buy a fully cooked pot roast or deli chicken for the filling.
- Buy a bag of carrots, peas, and corn—use them frozen.
- Forget about making a cream sauce; use condensed cream of celery soup instead.
- Add a jar of drained sliced mushrooms to the filling for easy richness.

Then let it bake—and enjoy the compliments!

SuperQuick
CHICKEN ENCHILADAS
Prep **10 MINUTES**   *Cook* **20 MINUTES**

1½   cups taco sauce

1   cup shredded cooked chicken

1   cup nacho and taco shredded cheese or mild Cheddar (4 ounces)

¾   cup plain nonfat yogurt

½   cup quartered zucchini slices

3   tablespoons minced jalapeño chile peppers

6   (6-inch) corn tortillas, warmed

2   tablespoons chopped fresh cilantro

Why not stop by the deli counter and pick up a rotisserie chicken for these enchiladas? You'll have enough chicken left over for at least one tasty brown-bag sandwich.

LET'S BEGIN Preheat the oven to 400°F. Pour ½ cup of the taco sauce into a shallow baking dish. Combine the chicken, ½ cup of the cheese, ½ cup of the yogurt, the zucchini, and chile peppers.

ROLL 'EM UP Spread ¼ cup of the chicken mixture down the center of each tortilla. Roll up and place seam side down in the baking dish. Pour the remaining taco sauce over the tortillas and spread to cover evenly. Sprinkle with the remaining cheese.

INTO THE OVEN Cover and bake for 20 minutes, or until the enchiladas are heated through and the cheese melts. Top with the remaining yogurt and sprinkle with the cilantro.

Makes 3 servings

Per serving: 385 calories, 22g protein, 42g carbohydrates, 15g fat, 7g saturated fat, 50mg cholesterol, 1,219mg sodium

Microwave in Minutes

MICROWAVE ENCHILADAS IN HALF THE TIME!

Assemble as directed in the recipe above, but do not sprinkle the top with the ½ cup cheese. Cover the dish with plastic wrap, microwave on High for 6 minutes. Remove the plastic wrap, sprinkle with the ½ cup cheese, and microwave 1 minute longer, or until the cheese melts and the enchiladas are heated through.

TOSTADO GRANDE
Prep **10 MINUTES**   *Cook* **17 MINUTES**

1   package (11 ounces) refrigerated biscuits

1   package (6 ounces) corn chips, crushed

1   cup sour cream

1   bottle (8 ounces) creamy Italian dressing

1½   tablespoons all-purpose flour

¾   pound cooked turkey or chicken, cut into bite-size pieces (2½ cups)

1   can (4 ounces) chopped green chiles, drained

⅓   cup sliced black olives

Toppings: shredded lettuce, shredded Cheddar cheese, chopped tomatoes, sliced scallions, diced green bell pepper, and/or sliced black olives

Traditionally made with a deep-fried flour tortilla, the refrigerated biscuits in this recipe eliminate the frying and cut down on your kitchen time. Save more time by using cooked deli chicken or turkey.

LET'S BEGIN Preheat the oven to 400°F. Pat the biscuits into the bottom of a 15½ × 10½-inch baking pan. Sprinkle the biscuits with the chips, mounding them on both sides. Bake for 10 minutes.

TOP 'EM Meanwhile, combine the sour cream, dressing, and flour in a large bowl and stir to mix well. Stir in the turkey, chiles, and olives. Spread the mixture evenly over the baked chips, leaving a 1-inch border.

INTO THE OVEN Bake 7 minutes longer, or until the edges are browned. Cut into squares and serve with any or all of the toppings.

Makes 8 servings
Per serving (without toppings): 460 calories, 17g protein, 35g carbohydrates, 28g fat, 7g saturated fat, 43mg cholesterol, 1,177mg sodium

SuperQuick
CHICKEN NUGGETS

Prep **10 MINUTES**   *Cook* **10 MINUTES**

1¼ pounds boneless,
skinless chicken breasts,
cut into 2-inch pieces

1 packet seasoned chicken
coating mix

Barbecue sauce

Super-quick is right! Just three easy ingredients and you are well on your way to fun-to-eat chicken nuggets. Round out the meal with steamed green beans, sliced tomatoes, and your favorite potato salad.

LET'S BEGIN Preheat the oven to 400°F. Place the chicken pieces in a colander, rinse with cold water, and drain.

COAT 'EM Place the coating mix in a resealable plastic bag, add the chicken in several batches, and shake to coat. Discard any remaining coating mix.

INTO THE OVEN Place the chicken pieces in a single layer in a jelly-roll pan. Bake for 10 to 15 minutes, or until the chicken is cooked through. Serve with the barbecue sauce.

Makes 6 servings

Per serving: 160 calories, 24g protein, 9g carbohydrates, 3g fat, 1g saturated fat, 55mg cholesterol, 350mg sodium

VICHYSSOISE TART

Prep **15 MINUTES**   *Cook* **38 MINUTES**

6   large eggs

½   teaspoon onion salt

2   cups mashed potatoes,
     prepared from instant
     potato flakes, cooled

1   cup thinly sliced leeks

2   tablespoons water

1   can (5 ounces) chunk
     chicken

Skim or low-fat milk
     (about 15 tablespoons)

1   tablespoon lemon juice

Dill sprigs (optional)

Vichyssoise—that cold, creamy potato and leek soup from France—has gone one better. It's now turned into a tempting tart. A generous amount of eggs makes the custard filling silky smooth.

LET'S BEGIN Preheat the oven to 375°F. Coat a 9-inch pie plate with cooking spray and set aside. Combine 1 egg and the onion salt in a large bowl and stir to mix well. Add the potatoes and stir until well blended. Spread the mixture over the bottom and up the sides of the prepared pan.

FIX IT FAST Combine the leeks with the water in a medium saucepan. Cover and cook over medium heat, stirring occasionally, for 8 to 10 minutes, or until the leeks are tender; discard liquid. Drain the liquid from the chicken into a measuring cup and add enough milk to make 1 cup. Set aside. Arrange the chicken and the leeks on top of the prepared potato crust.

INTO THE OVEN Combine the lemon juice, the remaining eggs, and the milk mixture in a large bowl and whisk until blended. Pour over the chicken and leeks. Bake for 30 to 40 minutes, or until the tart is puffed and a knife inserted near the center comes out clean. Garnish with the dill sprigs, if you wish.

Makes 6 servings

Per serving: 135 calories, 13g protein, 5g carbohydrates, 7g fat, 2g saturated fat, 227mg cholesterol, 331mg sodium

---

Food Facts

AMERICA'S LOVE AFFAIR WITH QUICHE

Remember quiche? It's a dish that originated in the Alsace-Lorraine region of France. The first recipes for quiche didn't appear in American cookbooks until the 1951 edition of *Joy of Cooking*.

We have the late Julia Child and her television program *The French Chef* to thank for truly introducing America to quiche and its varied possibilities. She called quiche "just a custard in fancy dress." And with those words, we learned that quiche was no big deal to prepare, but oh so delicious.

Before long, every conceivable version began appearing in cookbooks and in women's magazines. We embraced quiche wholeheartedly, to forever bake and enjoy!

Snapper Veracruz, page 86

Fisherman's Specials

Does your family love eating fish more than you love cooking it? Then read on—this chapter has some great discoveries in store for you. Nothing's easier (or faster!) than saucing red snapper with salsa Veracruz style and serving supper minutes later. Another night, impress your guests by serving a whole trout flavored inside and out with fresh lemon that takes only 30 minutes from start to finish. In fact, all of our recipes in this chapter are quick and simple to fix: Season fish or sauce it, slide it into the oven, and walk away. You'll even find an invaluable guide showing in an instant which fish to substitute for what, just in case your fish market doesn't have the fish a recipe calls for. How easy it is, thanks to these recipes, easy-to-buy fresh fish, and your oven.

SALMON WITH TOMATOES, SPINACH & MUSHROOMS

Prep **10 MINUTES** *Cook* **20 MINUTES**

4	salmon fillets (4 ounces each)
2	cups chopped fresh spinach
1	cup sliced mushrooms
1	medium tomato, chopped
⅓	cup sun-dried tomato vinaigrette

Omega-3 rich salmon is not only very good for you but it tastes good too. Sun-dried tomato vinaigrette adds just the right amount of zing without extra work. Cut down on your kitchen time by buying presliced mushrooms.

LET'S BEGIN Preheat the oven to 375°F. Coat a large baking dish with cooking spray and place the salmon skin sides down in the dish.

INTO THE OVEN Combine the spinach, mushrooms, tomato, and vinaigrette in a large bowl and stir to mix well. Spoon the mixture over the salmon. Bake for 20 to 25 minutes, or until the fish flakes easily when tested with a fork.

Makes 4 servings

Per serving: 190 calories, 24g protein, 5g carbohydrates, 7g fat, 1g saturated fat, 60mg cholesterol, 320mg sodium

Cooking Basics

HOW TO COOK A WHOLE FISH

There are several reasons why cooking the fish with bones and all is the best choice. The bones keep the fish moist and flavorful. And best of all, it is the least expensive way to purchase fish.

Here are some guidelines to help you through the process of cooking a whole fish in the oven.

HOW MUCH TO BUY For four people, you will need a whole fish weighing about 3 pounds.

CHOOSING THE RIGHT FISH Here is a short list of wonderful fish for cooking whole: black sea bass, striped bass, mackerel, pompano, red snapper, salmon, tilapia, tilefish, trout, and sea trout. Ask to have the fish dressed (cleaned with the tail and head left on) or pan-dressed (cleaned with the head and tail removed).

TIME TO ROAST A whole 3-pound fish will take approximately 35 to 40 minutes at 425°F.

HERE'S HOW Place a layer of sliced carrots and onions in the bottom of a shallow roasting pan. Season with salt and pepper and drizzle with oil. Roast for 10 minutes. Put some lemon slices and fresh parsley sprigs (or other herb) in the cav-ity of the fish. Place the fish on top of the vegetables. Rub the fish with oil and drizzle the fish and vegetables with some dry white wine or broth.

HOW TO TELL IF THE FISH IS DONE Insert a fork or small knife into the thickest part of the fish to see if it is opaque throughout. Or insert an instant-read thermometer: The temperature should read 140°F.

HOW TO SERVE IT Use two pancake spatulas to transfer the fish to a warm platter. Use a small knife to cut down through the skin until you reach the bones. Then use a spatula to lift up a portion of the flesh.

CRISPY OVEN FISH BAKE

Prep **15 MINUTES**   *Cook* **20 MINUTES**

4   tablespoons olive oil

¼   cup chopped fresh basil

¼   cup chopped fresh tarragon

¼   cup chopped fresh thyme

¼   cup chopped fresh dill

6   5-ounce firm white fish fillets (cod, pollack, or snapper)

1   tablespoon green hot-pepper sauce

Salt

Ground black pepper

Green hot-pepper sauce adds just the right zip to this dish. The recipe showcases the fabulous flavor of fresh herbs, so if you happen to have an herb garden or live near a farmers' market, take full advantage and enjoy them here.

LET'S BEGIN Preheat the oven to 350°F. Place 2 tablespoons of the oil in a large baking pan and place it in the oven for 15 minutes.

SEASON & SPICE Meanwhile, combine the basil, tarragon, thyme, and dill in a shallow dish and set aside. Coat the fish with the hot-pepper sauce and the remaining 2 tablespoons olive oil. Season to taste with the salt and pepper. Place each fillet in the herb mixture and coat both sides completely.

INTO THE OVEN Remove the baking pan from the oven and place the fish in the pan. Bake for 20 minutes, or until the fish flakes easily when tested with a fork.

Makes 6 servings

Per serving: 200 calories, 26g protein, 1g carbohydrates, 10g fat, 1g saturated fat, 61mg cholesterol, 142mg sodium

SuperQuick
CHEESY CATFISH

Prep **10 MINUTES**   *Cook* **10 MINUTES**

2   tablespoons butter or margarine

½   cup grated Parmesan cheese

¼   cup yellow cornmeal

¼   cup all-purpose flour

1   teaspoon paprika

½   teaspoon ground black pepper

2   pounds catfish fillets

Catfish is loved for its mild flavor and flaky, moist texture. Serve the fish with tartar sauce, wedges of fresh lemon, and thick, juicy slices of tomato.

LET'S BEGIN Preheat the oven to 400°F. Place the butter in a 13 × 9-inch baking pan and put in the oven to melt while the oven is heating. Remove the pan from the oven.

SEASON & SPICE Combine the Parmesan, cornmeal, flour, paprika, and pepper in a resealable plastic bag. Add the fillets, one at a time, and shake to coat with the mixture.

INTO THE OVEN Arrange the fillets in a single layer in the prepared pan, turning once to coat with the butter. Sprinkle the remaining Parmesan mixture over the fish. Bake for 10 to 15 minutes, or until golden brown and the fish flakes easily when tested with a fork.

Makes 4 servings

Per serving: 467 calories, 41g protein, 16g carbohydrates, 26g fat, 9g saturated fat, 132mg cholesterol, 317mg sodium

---

Cook to Cook

HOW DO YOU CHOOSE THE BEST FISH IN THE MARKET?

"I always keep in mind that fish is very perishable and therefore choose it very carefully. First off, *the fish counter should be spotless and odor-free.* When purchasing fish, let your eyes and nose be your guide. Firm fish that springs back when lightly pressed is very fresh, but there is a good chance that you will not be allowed to touch the fish. So a good visual inspection will do equally well.

The surface of whole *fish should glisten but not look or be slimy.* Ask the fishmonger to show you the gills. They should be bright red and look very fresh. The eyes of the fish should not be sunken, but don't worry if they are clouded over, as this is not always a sign of an old fish.

When choosing fish fillets and steaks that are sold in plastic packages, look for moist-looking and firm-feeling flesh. And be sure the flesh does not have any gaps.

Clams, oysters, and mussels must be purchased live because they deteriorate very quickly as soon as they die. Avoid any with broken shells or those that feel unusually heavy. There is a good chance that their shells are filled with sand."

SNAPPER VERACRUZ

Prep **10 MINUTES**   *Cook* **20 MINUTES**

4	red snapper or halibut fillets (6 ounces each)
1	tablespoon lime or lemon juice
1	can (8 ounces) stewed tomatoes
¼	cup sliced pimiento-stuffed green olives
2	tablespoons hot salsa or 1 tablespoon minced jalapeño chile pepper
1	teaspoon ground coriander
½	teaspoon dried oregano
1½	cups four-cheese Mexican shredded cheese blend (6 ounces)

Lime wedges (optional)

Here's an easy trick for getting the most juice out of a lemon or lime. Put the fruit on the counter and roll it back and forth, pressing down hard as you go. It loosens up the juice so you are sure to get every tasty drop.

LET'S BEGIN Preheat the oven to 350°F. Place the fish in a single layer in a shallow baking dish. Drizzle the lime juice over the fish.

MAKE IT SAUCY Combine the tomatoes, olives, salsa, coriander, and oregano in a small bowl and stir to mix well. Spoon over the fish.

INTO THE OVEN Bake for 20 minutes, or until the fish is opaque. Sprinkle the cheese over the fish. Let stand for 3 minutes or until the cheese melts. Serve with lime wedges, if you wish.

Makes 4 servings

Per serving: 330 calories, 39g protein, 6g carbohydrates, 16g fat, 9g saturated fat, 91mg cholesterol, 714mg sodium

SuperQuick
LEMON TROUT

Prep **15 MINUTES**   _Cook_ **15 MINUTES**

4   whole dressed trout
     (8 ounces each)

4   tablespoons all-purpose
     flour

1   teaspoon dried thyme

Salt

Ground black pepper

2   lemons, cut into sixteen
     ¼-inch-thick slices

1   cup vegetable broth

½   teaspoon grated lemon
     zest

1   cup instant brown rice

"Dressed" fish has been scaled and cleaned with the head and tail left on. If you prefer, ask your fishmonger for pan-dressed fish, meaning the head and tail will be removed.

LET'S BEGIN Preheat the oven to 450°F. Coat a large baking pan with cooking spray and set it aside. Rub the outside of each trout with 1 tablespoon of the flour and sprinkle the inside cavities evenly with the thyme and the salt and pepper to taste. Place 4 lemon slices inside the cavity of each trout.

INTO THE OVEN Place the trout in the prepared baking pan and spray them lightly with cooking spray. Bake for 15 to 20 minutes, or until the fish flakes easily when tested with a fork.

FLUFF IT UP Meanwhile, bring the vegetable broth and lemon zest to a boil in a medium saucepan over high heat. Stir in the rice and return to a boil. Reduce the heat, cover, and simmer for 5 minutes. Remove from the heat and let stand for 5 minutes, or until the liquid is absorbed. Fluff with a fork before serving. Serve the rice with the trout.

**Makes 4 servings**
Per serving: 400 calories, 39g protein, 34g carbohydrates, 12g fat, 2g saturated fat, 99mg cholesterol, 416mg sodium

CRABMEAT IN PHYLLO SHELLS

Prep **10 MINUTES**   *Cook* **10 MINUTES**

½   cup whole berry cranberry sauce

⅓   cup cream cheese, softened

¼   cup minced crabmeat

2   tablespoons sliced scallion, white and green parts

15   individual frozen mini-phyllo shells, thawed

Keep in mind that it takes about 30 minutes for cream cheese to soften. And be sure to pick through the crabmeat to remove any shell or cartilage.

LET'S BEGIN Preheat the oven to 375°F. Place the cranberry sauce in a small bowl and beat with a fork or a wire whisk until it is smooth.

FILL & BAKE Combine the cream cheese, crabmeat, and scallion in a small bowl and stir to mix well. Fill each phyllo shell with about 1 teaspoon of the cream cheese mixture and top with ½ teaspoon of the cranberry sauce.

INTO THE OVEN Place the phyllo shells on a baking sheet and bake for 10 minutes, or until heated through.

> **Makes 15 servings**
>
> *Per serving: 49 calories, 1g protein, 6g carbohydrates, 2g fat, 1g saturated fat, 8mg cholesterol, 54mg sodium*

EASY FISH & VEGETABLE BAKE

Prep **10 MINUTES**   *Cook* **30 MINUTES**

1   pound cod fillets

1   package (16 ounces) broccoli stir-fry vegetable blend

1   teaspoon dried parsley

1½   teaspoons salt

1   teaspoon lemon pepper seasoning

½   cup vegetable juice cocktail

¼   cup grated Parmesan cheese

Be sure to check the fish for doneness after 25 minutes. It should easily flake with a fork, and the flesh should be translucent, not white and dry looking.

LET'S BEGIN Preheat the oven to 400°F. Line a 13 × 9-inch pan with heavy-duty foil.

SEASON & BAKE Place the fish in the pan and top with the vegetable blend. Sprinkle with the parsley, salt, and lemon pepper. Pour the juice over the fish and sprinkle with the cheese.

INTO THE OVEN Cover and bake for 30 minutes, or until the vegetables are crisp-tender and the fish flakes easily when tested with a fork.

> **Makes 4 servings**
>
> *Per serving: 155 calories, 24g protein, 9g carbohydrates, 2g fat, 1g saturated fat, 53mg cholesterol, 1,133mg sodium*

FISHERMAN'S WHARF CRAB BAKE

Prep **20 MINUTES**   *Cook* **20 MINUTES**

The secret flavoring in this delicious sauce is beau monde seasoning—a perfect blend of sale, onion, and celery seed. Great for sprinkling on meats and vegetables too.

1	cup crabmeat
2	tablespoons dry sherry
2	tablespoons butter or margarine
2	teaspoons arrowroot
1	cup light cream
½	teaspoon dried beau monde seasoning
¼	teaspoon dry mustard
⅛	teaspoon ground black pepper
1	cup white mushrooms, sliced
½	cup shredded Swiss cheese (2 ounces)
1	hard-cooked egg, chopped
2	teaspoons dried parsley
⅛	teaspoon paprika

LET'S BEGIN Preheat the oven to 350° F. Combine the crabmeat and sherry in a small bowl and toss to coat. Set aside.

FLASH INTO THE PAN Melt the butter in a large saucepan over medium heat and stir in the arrowroot. Gradually stir in the cream, then add the beau monde seasoning, mustard, and pepper. Cook, stirring constantly, for 3 minutes, until the sauce comes to a boil and thickens. Remove the pan from the heat and stir in the mushrooms, cheese, egg, parsley, and crabmeat mixture.

BAKE & SERVE Spoon the mixture into 4 buttered ramekins or a 1-quart casserole. Bake for 12 to 15 minutes, or until bubbly and heated through. Sprinkle with the paprika before serving.

Makes 4 servings

Per serving: 375 calories, 21g protein, 5g carbohydrates, 30g fat, 18g saturated fat, 200mg cholesterol, 458mg sodium

---

On the Menu

Place some clean newspapers on your picnic table, put out a pile of napkins with flatware rolled up inside, and stack your favorite plates. It's time to have a crab bake!

Sliced Tomato and Red Onion Salad

Blue Cheese Dressing

Fisherman's Wharf Crab Bake

Warm Buttermilk Biscuits

Oven Fries

Deep Dish Peach Pie

Rich Vanilla Ice Cream

Lemon Iced Tea

ACAPULCO BAKED FISH

Prep **5 MINUTES** *Cook* **12 MINUTES**

1½   pounds halibut, cod,
      scrod, or hake, cut into
      1-inch pieces

2   tablespoons lemon juice

1   cup chunky-style salsa

1½   cups four-cheese
      Mexican shredded
      cheese blend (6 ounces)

Just four ingredients and you are on your way to a super-tasty main dish. Round out the meal with steamed spinach and rice, then end on a tropical note with mango or passion fruit sorbet.

LET'S BEGIN Preheat the oven to 425°F. Arrange the fish in a single layer in a shallow baking dish and drizzle with the lemon juice.

MAKE IT SAUCY Top with the salsa and then with the cheese.

INTO THE OVEN Bake for 12 minutes, or until the fish flakes easily when tested with a fork.

Makes 6 servings

Per serving: 247 calories, 30g protein, 4g carbohydrates, 12g fat, 6g saturated fat, 62mg cholesterol, 565mg sodium

---

Cooking Basics

A SIMPLE WAY TO MAKE SMART FISH SUBSTITUTIONS

Sometimes you have your heart set on buying a particular fish, but when you arrive at the market you find that your choice is either not available or not the freshest-looking fish on display. Don't despair! Here is a list of fish that are interchangeable—depending on how you plan to use them—based on their oil content. Just find which group the fish you wanted to buy is in, then choose any other from that same group.

LEAN cod and scrod, flounder, grouper, haddock, hake, halibut, monkfish, pike, pollack, red and pink snapper, sea bass, sole, tilefish, turbot.

MODERATELY LEAN bluefish, catfish, mahi-mahi, rainbow trout, striped bass, swordfish, yellowfin tuna.

OILY bluefin tuna, butterfish, herring, lake trout, mackerel, pompano, salmon, shad, and whitefish.

CRAB & ARTICHOKE BAKE

Prep **20 MINUTES**   *Cook* **25 MINUTES**

6	tablespoons butter or margarine
1	cup sliced mushrooms
3	tablespoons all-purpose flour
¼	cup fresh-squeezed lemon juice
1	cup whole milk
12	ounces crabmeat
1	cup canned artichoke hearts, drained and quartered
¼	cup diced red bell peppers
¼	cup grated Parmesan cheese
2	tablespoons fresh chopped parsley
¼	teaspoon salt
⅛	teaspoon ground white pepper
¼	cups panko (Japanese bread crumbs)

Panko are very special bread crumbs—they stay extremely crispy and are very light. Look for them in many large supermarkets in the aisle with Asian ingredients and in specialty food stores.

LET'S BEGIN Preheat the oven to 375°F. Heat 1 tablespoon of the butter in a small skillet over medium heat. Add the mushrooms and cook for 5 minutes, or until they are softened. Set the mushrooms aside.

MAKE IT SAUCY Heat 3 tablespoons of the butter in a medium saucepan over medium heat. Add the flour and cook, stirring constantly, for 1 minute. Stir in the lemon juice. Slowly add the milk, whisking constantly, until the mixture comes to a boil and thickens. Remove from the heat.

INTO THE OVEN Combine the mushrooms, crabmeat, artichokes, bell pepper, cheese, parsley, salt, and pepper in a medium bowl. Add the milk mixture and stir to mix well. Divide the mixture evenly among 4 individual casseroles or soufflé dishes. Sprinkle the tops with the bread crumbs and drizzle with the remaining butter. Bake for 15 to 20 minutes, or until lightly browned and bubbling.

Makes 4 servings
Per serving: 360 calories, 23g protein, 17g carbohydrates, 23g fat, 11g saturated fat, 125mg cholesterol, 680mg sodium

SHRIMP PIE

Prep **25 MINUTES** *Cook* **45 MINUTES**

1½ cups long-grain parboiled white rice

3 tablespoons butter

2 medium onions, diced

2 cups medium peeled shrimp

2 tablespoons diced pimientos

1 tablespoon dried parsley

1 can (10¾ ounces) cream of mushroom soup, undiluted

1½ tablespoons lemon juice

Salt

Ground black pepper

Save time by purchasing shrimp that have already been peeled.

LET'S BEGIN Preheat the oven to 350°F. Cook the rice according to package directions. Meanwhile, heat 1½ tablespoons of the butter in a medium saucepan over medium heat. Add half of the onions and cook, stirring often, for 3 minutes, or until it begins to soften. Add the shrimp and cook for 5 minutes, or until they turn pink. Set aside.

LAYER IT EASY Combine the remaining butter and onion, the pimientos, parsley, and rice in a large bowl and stir to mix well. Press this mixture on the bottom and up the sides of a large deep-dish pie plate (10-inch or larger) or a large casserole. Spoon the shrimp mixture on top of the rice.

MAKE IT SAUCY Combine the soup, lemon juice, and the salt and pepper to taste in a medium saucepan and cook over medium heat, stirring occasionally, until the mixture boils. Pour the soup mixture over the shrimp, cover, and bake for 30 to 40 minutes, or until heated through.

Makes 8 servings

Per serving: 243 calories, 8g protein, 35g carbohydrates, 8g fat, 3g saturated fat, 44mg cholesterol, 365mg sodium

Cook to Cook

WHAT IS YOUR FAVORITE SEAFOOD TO USE IN A FISH PIE?

"Sometimes I like to use just one favorite fish or shellfish, and at other times I like to mix things up a bit. **There are no rules, and you can't really go wrong** with any combination you choose. Here are some of my favorites:

Salmon is such a delicious fish that I like to use it by itself in a fish pie. When I want to combine fish and shellfish, I go with this mix: **monkfish or red snapper** fillets with mussels, shrimp, and cod or scrod.

When I want to pull out all the stops for a special occasion, I use **lobster chunks.**

Sometimes I want my pie to be just about shellfish, and I buy a mix of **sea scallops, medium shrimp,** a small amount of crabmeat, and small clams, such as littlenecks. Other times, I keep it simple and use just bay scallops and shrimp. "

Boston Baked Beans, page 113

Off to the Side

Remember when it was hard to get everyone to eat their vegetables? Luckily those days are gone, thanks to creative techniques for growing, seasoning, spicing, and serving healthy vegetables. Here you'll find some all-time favorites: green bean casserole topped with fried onions, a Boston bean bake, and Potatoes Au Gratin. But that's not all. Try some of the new favorite ways with vegetable sides too. Stir a corn pudding, stuff tomatoes with fresh herbs, or bake a batch of zesty fries. We've added another popular side—fresh-from-the-oven breads, including buttermilk biscuits the way they bake them in the South and soda bread just the way it's baked in Ireland. Naturally, these are all fast to fix and just slide into the oven.

BROCCOLI CASHEW CASSEROLE

Prep **25 MINUTES**   *Cook* **45 MINUTES**

8   ounces linguine

3   tablespoons butter or
      margarine

⅓   cup all-purpose flour

2   cups milk

2   cups shredded Swiss
      cheese (8 ounces)

¾   cup shredded Parmesan
      cheese (3 ounces)

2   tablespoons poppy seeds

1   teaspoon onion salt

½   teaspoon ground black
      pepper

1   large egg

1   package (16 ounces)
      frozen chopped broccoli,
      thawed

1½   cups cashews

Since the linguine in the casserole is cooked twice, there is a chance it will get overcooked in the oven. So we suggest slightly undercooking it when first cooked on the stove.

LET'S BEGIN Preheat the oven to 350°F. Cook the linguine according to package directions. Drain and keep warm.

MAKE IT SAUCY Melt the butter in a medium saucepan over medium-high heat. Stir in the flour. Gradually stir in the milk and bring to a boil, stirring constantly, until thick and smooth. Add the Swiss, ½ cup of the Parmesan, the poppy seeds, onion salt, and pepper. Remove the saucepan from the heat. Break the egg into a small bowl and beat it lightly with a fork. Stir a small amount of the hot milk mixture into the beaten egg. Stir the egg mixture back into the milk mixture.

TOSS & BAKE Combine the linguine, the milk mixture, broccoli, and cashews in a large bowl and toss to combine. Transfer to a greased 2-quart baking dish and sprinkle with the remaining Parmesan cheese. Bake for 35 minutes, or until bubbly and heated through.

Makes 6 servings

Per serving: 691 calories, 34g protein, 54g carbohydrates, 39g fat, 17g saturated fat, 54mg cholesterol, 871mg sodium

Sweet Corn Pudding

Prep **15 MINUTES**   *Cook* **40 MINUTES**

½ cup masa harina flour (Mexican corn masa mix)

4 tablespoons cold butter or margarine, cut into pieces

2 tablespoons shortening

2 cups frozen whole kernel corn, thawed

3 tablespoons cold water

¼ cup sugar

3 tablespoons yellow cornmeal

2 tablespoons evaporated milk

¼ teaspoon baking powder

¼ teaspoon salt

1 teaspoon chili powder (optional)

Masa harina, *Spanish for "dough flour,"* is traditionally used for making corn tortillas. It is made with dried corn kernels that have been cooked in limewater, soaked overnight, and then ground into fine meal. Here it's used in that forever popular Southwestern corn pudding.

LET'S BEGIN Preheat the oven to 350°F. Coat a 9-inch pie plate with cooking spray and set aside. Combine the flour, butter, and shortening in a food processor and pulse until well combined. Add the corn and water and process until the corn is coarsely chopped.

STIR IT TOGETHER Combine the sugar, cornmeal, milk, baking powder, and salt in a medium bowl. Add the corn mixture and stir until mixed well. Spread into the prepared pie plate. Sprinkle with the chili powder, if you wish.

INTO THE OVEN Bake for 40 to 50 minutes, or until firm and lightly browned around the edges. Cool on a wire rack for 15 minutes before cutting into wedges.

Makes 8 servings

Per serving: 185 calories, 3g protein, 23g carbohydrates, 10g fat, 4g saturated fat, 17mg cholesterol, 130mg sodium

DOUBLE CHEDDAR GREEN BEAN CASSEROLE

Prep **5 MINUTES**   *Cook* **35 MINUTES**

1   can (10¾ ounces)
     condensed Cheddar
     cheese soup, undiluted

¾   cup milk

1½   cups shredded Cheddar
     cheese (6 ounces)

1   package (16 ounces)
     frozen cut green beans,
     thawed, or 4 cups fresh,
     cooked and drained

1⅓   cups Cheddar french-
     fried onions

Calling all Cheddar cheese lovers! Get your Cheddar fix with this easy casserole. You can bake it several hours ahead, then gently reheat it in a warm oven.

LET'S BEGIN Preheat the oven to 350°F. Combine the soup, milk, and 1 cup of the cheese in a 1½-quart baking dish and stir to mix well. Add the beans and ⅔ cup of the fried onions and stir to combine.

INTO THE OVEN Bake for 30 minutes, or until heated through. Remove the dish from the oven and stir the mixture well.

TOP IT OFF Sprinkle with the remaining cheese and fried onions. Bake 5 minutes longer, or until the onions are golden.

Makes 6 servings

Per serving: 287 calories, 11g protein, 16g carbohydrates, 20g fat, 10g saturated fat, 39mg cholesterol, 700mg sodium

HONEY BAKED RED ONIONS

Prep **10 MINUTES**   *Cook* **1 HOUR**

3   large red onions (about 1 pound each)

¼   cup water

⅓   cup honey

3   tablespoons butter or margarine, melted

1   teaspoon paprika (preferably sweet Hungarian)

1   teaspoon ground coriander

⅛   teaspoon cayenne pepper

½   teaspoon salt

This is a smart recipe. To guarantee that the onions will be nice and tender, they are first steamed in the oven. Then they are glazed twice with a spiced-up honey mixture and baked until tender, but not falling apart.

LET'S BEGIN Preheat the oven to 350°F. Peel the onions and cut them in half crosswise. Place them cut side down in a single layer in a shallow baking dish.

INTO THE OVEN Pour the water over the onions, cover, and bake for 30 minutes. Remove the pan from the oven and turn the onions cut side up.

BASTE & GLAZE Combine remaining ingredients in a small bowl and stir to mix well. Spoon half of the honey mixture over the onions. Return to the oven and bake, uncovered, for 15 minutes. Baste the onions with the remaining honey mixture and bake 15 minutes longer, or until tender.

Makes 6 servings
Per serving: 179 calories, 3g protein, 28g carbohydrates, 6g fat, 3g saturated fat, 16mg cholesterol, 265mg sodium

OVEN ROASTED POTATOES

Prep **10 MINUTES**   *Cook* **30 MINUTES**

1⅓   pounds golden-fleshed potatoes (about 4 medium)

2   tablespoons olive oil

2   tablespoons chopped fresh rosemary or 2 teaspoons dried

4   garlic cloves, minced

½   teaspoon salt

¼   teaspoon ground black pepper

1   medium red bell pepper, cut into 1-inch squares

Golden-fleshed potatoes, such as Yukon Gold, are prized for their beautiful buttery yellow color and creamy texture. They're great mashed, gratinéed, boiled, or baked.

LET'S BEGIN Preheat the oven to 475°F. Cut the potatoes into 1½-inch cubes.

TOSS 'EM Place all the ingredients in a large roasting pan and toss to coat.

INTO THE OVEN Arrange in a single layer and bake 30 to 35 minutes, until the potatoes are tender and lightly browned, stirring occasionally.

Makes 4 servings

Per serving: 235 calories, 4g protein, 40g carbohydrates, 7g fat, 1g saturated fat, 0mg cholesterol, 306mg sodium

---

Cooking Basics

A GUIDE TO NEW FINDS IN THE POTATO BIN

One potato . . . two potatoes . . . hundreds of potatoes around the world. One easy way through the potato maze is to remember that potatoes are classified according to their starch content, which relates to the ones that are best for boiling, mashing, baking, or frying.

High-starch potatoes, such as russets, are the best for baking, mashing, or deep-frying. They are perfect for turning into oven fries and baking into gratins, as they hold their shape well. They get very crisp on the outside and wonderfully creamy on the inside.

Medium-starch potatoes are also

called all-purpose potatoes. They can be baked, mashed, or fried. They are a little moister than russets and can also be boiled. Yukon Golds, with their buttery yellow flesh, are a very popular variety.

Low-starch potatoes are very firm-textured. They are sometimes referred to as boiling potatoes or waxy potatoes. Creamers and fingerlings are two very popular types of low-starch potatoes and are great for barbecuing, potato salads, oven roasting whole, and steaming. They hold their shape extremely well, even when boiled.

New potatoes are simply young or small potatoes, with waxy flesh and

thin skins. They hold up well when boiled and tossed into potato salads. They're also small enough to cook and serve whole and are especially great for pan-roasting in the oven.

The new potato bin has been appearing in many farmers' markets and in specialty food stores lately. A few groups that stand out: those red-fleshed potatoes (the huckleberry with red skin and flesh, and the blossom with more pinkish skin and flesh), which look great in a potato salad; and the all-blue Peruvian potatoes, which range from bluish purple to purple-black and are great for boiling and serving with steaks or chops.

ZIPPY OVEN FRIES

Prep **10 MINUTES**   *Cook* **25 MINUTES**

2   cups french-fried onions, finely crushed

½   cup grated Parmesan cheese

1   pound baking potatoes, cut into ¼-inch wedges

3   tablespoons melted butter or vegetable oil

2   tablespoons hot-pepper sauce, at room temperature

Zesty Ketchup (see recipe)

These oven-fried potatoes are cheesy, crispy, and oniony all rolled into one—without a lot of work. Make lots . . . they disappear fast.

LET'S BEGIN Preheat the oven to 400°F. Coat a large baking pan with cooking spray and set aside. Place the fried onions in a resealable plastic bag and use a rolling pin to finely crush them. Add the Parmesan and toss to mix well. Transfer to a shallow dish and set aside.

SEASON 'EM UP Place the potatoes, butter, and hot sauce in the resealable bag and toss to coat the potatoes. Then coat the potatoes with the fried onion mixture, pressing firmly to adhere.

INTO THE OVEN Arrange the potatoes in a single layer in the prepared pan and bake for 25 minutes, or until they are tender and golden brown. Serve with additional hot sauce or with Zesty Ketchup.

Makes 4 servings

Per serving: 385 calories, 6g protein, 31g carbohydrates, 26g fat, 10g saturated fat, 33mg cholesterol, 510mg sodium

ZESTY KETCHUP

Stir together 1 cup ketchup with 1 to 2 tablespoons hot sauce, spicing it as hot as you like.

Cook to Cook

HOW DO YOU MAKE SUCH GOOD SCALLOPED POTATOES?

"People always ask for my scalloped potato recipe, and they can't believe that it is simply a packaged scalloped potato mix with some add-ins.

Add cubes of honey-baked ham and a little Dijon mustard to flavor the sauce and a sprinkling of crushed butter-flavored crackers on top for a hearty side.

For something lighter, layer pre-washed *baby spinach leaves* with the potatoes and top with low-fat sour cream and fresh or dried dill.

For an instant make-over, top your potatoes with some toasted (dark) sesame oil and sesame seeds, paprika, and caraway seeds—or a Southwestern, Cajun, or Italian seasoning blend."

POTATOES AU GRATIN

Prep **15 MINUTES**   Cook **32 MINUTES**

2½ pounds baking potatoes (3 large), peeled and cut into ¼-inch slices

2 tablespoons butter or margarine

3 tablespoons all-purpose flour

2 cups milk

1 teaspoon salt

½ teaspoon ground black pepper

8 slices deli-sliced medium Cheddar cheese (½ ounce each)

Paprika (optional)

Using slices of cheese makes this tasty potato dish really easy to put together. You can even assemble it ahead of time and refrigerate it until you are ready to put it into the oven. Just be sure to allow a few extra minutes of baking if the gratin starts out cold from the refrigerator.

LET'S BEGIN Preheat the oven to 375°F. Coat a 2-quart baking dish with cooking spray and set aside. Cook the potatoes in boiling salted water for 6 to 8 minutes or until tender. Drain and set aside.

MAKE IT SAUCY Meanwhile, melt the butter in a medium saucepan over medium heat. Stir in the flour and cook, stirring constantly, for 1 minute. Slowly stir in the milk, salt, and pepper, and cook, stirring often, for 5 minutes, or until the sauce comes to a boil and thickens.

LAYER & BAKE Spoon ½ cup of the sauce into the prepared dish and top with half of the potatoes. Top with half of the remaining sauce and 4 slices of the cheese. Repeat with the remaining sauce, potatoes, and cheese. Sprinkle with the paprika, if you wish. Bake for 25 minutes, or until bubbly and heated through.

Makes 8 servings

Per serving: 258 calories, 11g protein, 30g carbohydrates, 11g fat, 7g saturated fat, 32mg cholesterol, 507mg sodium

SUPER SKINS

Prep **5 MINUTES**   *Cook* **15 MINUTES**

6   large baking potatoes, baked

2   tablespoons vegetable oil

1   jar (15 ounces) cheese dip, heated

¼   cup bacon bits

½   cup sour cream

¼   cup sliced scallions

Prepared cheese dip makes quick work of these tasty filled potato skins. We find that a grapefruit knife is a very easy way to remove the potato flesh, leaving an evenly thick shell.

LET'S BEGIN Preheat the oven to 375°F. Cut the potatoes in half lengthwise. Scoop out the centers (and reserve for another use), leaving ¼-inch-thick shells. Cut the shells in half crosswise.

INTO THE OVEN Arrange the shells, skin sides down, on a baking pan and brush the insides lightly with the oil. Bake for 15 minutes, or until golden brown.

TOP 'EM OFF Top the potatoes evenly with the cheese dip, bacon bits, sour cream, and scallions.

Makes 24 servings

Per serving: 100 calories, 3g protein, 9g carbohydrates, 6g fat, 3g saturated fat, 15mg cholesterol, 300mg sodium

YANKEE SWEET POTATOES

Prep **15 MINUTES**   *Cook* **1 HOUR**

2   **cans (16 ounces) sweet potatoes in light syrup, drained**

1   **cup peeled, cored, and thinly sliced apples**

½   **cup dried cranberries**

½   **cup light brown sugar, firmly packed**

2   **tablespoons butter or margarine**

2   **teaspoons pumpkin pie spice**

¼   **cup walnut or pecan halves (optional)**

You can enjoy some of the best flavors of Thanksgiving any time of year with this fruity and warmly spiced sweet potato casserole. Serve with roasted chicken or roasted turkey breast.

LET'S BEGIN Preheat the oven to 325°F. Cut the potatoes crosswise into ½-inch-thick slices. Arrange half of the potatoes in a shallow 1½-quart casserole. Top with the apples, then with the remaining potatoes. Set aside.

LAYER IT EASY In a small microwaveable bowl, combine the cranberries, sugar, butter, and pumpkin pie spice. Microwave on High for 1 minute, or until the butter is melted. Stir to mix well. Spoon the cranberry mixture evenly over the potatoes and sprinkle with the nuts, if you wish.

INTO THE OVEN Cover and bake for 1 hour, or until hot and bubbly.

Makes 8 servings

Per serving: 290 calories, 1g protein, 54g carbohydrates, 9g fat, 4g saturated fat, 16mg cholesterol, 106mg sodium

MASHED POTATO BAKE

Prep **15 MINUTES**   *Cook* **50 MINUTES**

Here's a great way to cook potatoes for mashing several hours ahead. Cook and drain the potatoes, then put them in a microwaveable bowl, cover with plastic wrap, and refrigerate. When you are ready to mash them, microwave them on Medium-high until nice and hot, then continue with the recipe.

6	large baking potatoes
¼	cup milk
8	ounces cream cheese, softened
1	cup sour cream
1	teaspoon dried parsley flakes
½	teaspoon refrigerated crushed garlic, or ¼ teaspoon garlic powder
½	cup shredded Cheddar cheese (2 ounces)

LET'S BEGIN Peel the potatoes, cut into cubes, and cook in a large pot of salted water for 15 to 20 minutes, or until tender. Preheat the oven to 325°F.

MIX IT UP Drain the potatoes and place them in a large mixing bowl with the milk, cream cheese, sour cream, parsley, and garlic. Beat with an electric mixer on medium-high speed until the mixture is smooth.

INTO THE OVEN Spoon the potatoes into a lightly greased 12 × 8-inch baking dish. Cover and bake for 30 to 40 minutes, or until heated through. Remove from the oven, uncover, and sprinkle with the Cheddar cheese. Bake 5 to 10 minutes longer, or until the cheese melts.

Makes 8 servings

Per serving: 247 calories, 7g protein, 15g carbohydrates, 18g fat, 11g saturated fat, 49mg cholesterol, 153mg sodium

CREAMED SPINACH

Prep **10 MINUTES**   *Cook* **30 MINUTES**

1   package (10 ounces)
      frozen chopped spinach

1   package (3 ounces)
      cream cheese, softened

1   tablespoon butter,
      melted

⅛   teaspoon ground nutmeg

1   tablespoon grated
      Parmesan cheese

Cream cheese is an easy way to put the "cream" into creamed spinach. Put the casserole together up to several hours ahead and refrigerate until you are ready to bake it.

LET'S BEGIN Preheat the oven to 350°F. Cook the spinach according to the package directions and drain well.

STIR IT UP Stir together the cream cheese, butter, and nutmeg in a large bowl. Add the spinach and stir to mix well.

INTO THE OVEN Spoon the mixture into a lightly greased 1-quart casserole. Sprinkle with the Parmesan, cover, and bake for 20 minutes, or until heated through.

INTO THE MICROWAVE To cook in the microwave instead of the oven, cover the casserole and cook on High for 3 minutes, or until heated through.

Makes 4 servings

Per serving: 122 calories, 4g protein, 4g carbohydrates, 11g fat, 7g saturated fat, 32mg cholesterol, 168mg sodium

BAKED TOMATOES WITH HERB TOPPING

Prep **15 MINUTES**   *Cook* **20 MINUTES + COOLING**

4	medium tomatoes
½	cup chopped fresh Italian parsley
½	cup chopped fresh basil
3	garlic cloves, minced
Salt	
Ground black pepper	
2	tablespoons olive oil
4	tablespoons grated Parmesan cheese

Do you know the fastest way to remove the pulp from tomatoes? Use a grapefruit knife to lift it out—but don't throw it away. Chop the pulp and toss it into tuna salad, pasta salad, or green salad.

LET'S BEGIN Preheat the oven to 350°F. Cut away the tops of the tomatoes and scoop out the seeds and pulp with a small spoon or grapefruit knife. Cut a thin slice from the bottoms and arrange the tomatoes in a baking dish.

STUFF 'EM Combine the parsley, basil, garlic, and salt and pepper to taste in a small bowl and stir to mix well. Spoon 2 tablespoons of the mixture into each tomato.

INTO THE OVEN Drizzle the tomatoes with the olive oil and top each with 1 tablespoon of the cheese. Bake for 20 minutes, or until the tomatoes are softened. Serve at room temperature.

Makes 4 servings

Per serving: 111 calories, 4g protein, 7g carbohydrates, 9g fat, 2g saturated fat, 4mg cholesterol, 160mg sodium

TWICE BAKED SQUASH

Prep **15 MINUTES**   *Cook* **45 MINUTES**

2	acorn squash (about ¾ pound each)
¼	cup water
8	tablespoons grated Parmesan cheese
1	cup low-fat cottage cheese
2	large eggs
½	cup instant potato flakes
½	cup minced scallions
1	teaspoon lemon juice
1	teaspoon salt
⅓	cup unseasoned croutons or stuffing cubes

Hard-skinned acorn squash falls into the category of winter squash and is a welcome sight in farmers' markets in early fall. To cut it in half easily, use a heavy chef's knife or a sturdy serrated knife.

LET'S BEGIN Preheat the oven to 350°F. Cut the squash in half, remove the seeds, and place in a large microwaveable dish. Add the water and cover the dish with plastic wrap, leaving an opening for a vent at one corner. Microwave on High for 10 minutes, or until the squash is tender. Remove the plastic wrap and drain off the water. Scoop the flesh from the squash into a medium bowl. Place the squash shells in a shallow baking dish and set aside.

STUFF & BAKE Mash the squash flesh and stir in 4 tablespoons of the Parmesan, the cottage cheese, eggs, potato flakes, scallions, lemon juice, and salt. Spoon the mixture into the squash shells and top with the remaining Parmesan and the croutons. Bake for 35 to 45 minutes, or until a knife inserted near the center comes out clean.

Makes 4 servings

Per serving: 225 calories, 17g protein, 27g carbohydrates, 6g fat, 3g saturated fat, 116mg cholesterol, 765mg sodium

---

Microwave in Minutes

SPEEDING UP ACORN SQUASH

Stuffed acorn squash brings back memories of Grandma's oven warming the kitchen for more than an hour as the aroma of roasted squash filled the air. Today you can save a lot of oven time by letting your microwave oven do some of the cooking.

Split a 1-pound acorn squash and remove the seeds. Place the two halves upside down in a microwaveable baking dish and microwave on High for 5 minutes. Turn the squash upright and microwave 3 to 6 minutes longer until tender. Transfer to an oven-safe baking dish, then stuff and roast in the oven just until browned.

Microwave your packaged stuffing mix following the package directions, then stir in the cooked sausage, stuff the squash, and finish it in a hot oven until golden.

SuperQuick
SPINACH CASSEROLE

Prep **10 MINUTES**   *Cook* **20 MINUTES**

1   package (10 ounces)
       frozen chopped spinach,
       thawed and squeezed dry

¾   cup ricotta cheese

1   garlic clove, minced, or
       ½ teaspoon garlic powder

½   teaspoon salt

¼   teaspoon ground black
       pepper

2   medium tomatoes, thinly
       sliced

½   cup shredded mozzarella
       cheese (2 ounces)

¼   cup shredded Parmesan
       cheese (1 ounce)

This is a tempting side dish for almost any simply roasted meat, fish, or poultry. Creamy spinach with vine-ripened tomatoes, using three different cheeses in one dish is simply fabulous!

LET'S BEGIN Preheat the oven to 350°F. Mix the first 5 ingredients in a medium bowl.

LAYER IT Spread half of the spinach mixture into an 8 × 8-inch baking dish and top with one of the sliced tomatoes. Repeat the layering with the remaining spinach mixture and tomato. Sprinkle the top with the mozzarella and the Parmesan.

INTO THE OVEN Bake for 20 minutes, or until heated through and the cheese melts.

Makes 4 servings

Per serving: 171 calories, 14g protein, 10g carbohydrates, 10g fat, 6g saturated fat, 33mg cholesterol, 442mg sodium

ITALIAN VEGETABLE BAKE

Prep **20 MINUTES**   *Bake* **1 HOUR 15 MINUTES**

1   can (28 ounces) whole tomatoes, coarsely chopped and liquid reserved

½   pound green beans, sliced

½   pound okra, cut into ½-inch pieces, or ½ package (10 ounces) frozen cut okra

1   medium onion, sliced

1   medium green bell pepper, finely chopped (¾ cup)

2   tablespoons lemon juice

1   tablespoon chopped fresh basil or 1 teaspoon dried, crumbled

1½   teaspoons fresh oregano leaves or ½ teaspoon dried, crumbled

1   medium zucchini, cut into 1-inch cubes

1   medium eggplant, peeled and cut into 1-inch cubes

2   tablespoons grated Parmesan cheese

Six different fresh vegetables from the farmers' market team up with canned tomatoes to make this delicious oven-roasted combo. The best part: You just slice, dice, and chop. The oven does the rest. Perfect to serve alongside pot roast, meat loaf, or grilled pork chops.

LET'S BEGIN Preheat the oven to 325°F. Mix the first 8 ingredients together in a large bowl. Transfer to a large baking dish. Cover and bake for 15 minutes.

BAKE IT Stir in the zucchini and eggplant. Cover and bake, stirring occasionally, 1 hour longer, or until the vegetables are tender. Sprinkle with the cheese.

Makes 8 servings

Per serving: 75 calories, 4g protein, 15g carbohydrates, 1g total fat, 0g saturated fat, 1mg cholesterol, 239mg sodium

BOSTON BAKED BEANS

Prep **10 MINUTES**   *Cook* **50 MINUTES**

Canned baked beans make quick work of preparing authentic-tasting Boston baked beans. For the best flavor, use strong, freshly brewed coffee.

1	teaspoon vegetable oil
1	medium onion, chopped
2	cans (16 ounces each) baked beans
½	cup brewed coffee
¼	cup honey
½	teaspoon mustard powder
¼	teaspoon ground black pepper

LET'S BEGIN Preheat the oven to 350°F. Heat the oil in a large skillet over medium heat. Add the onion and cook, stirring often, for 5 minutes, or until tender.

SEASON 'EM Transfer the onions to a 1½-quart casserole dish. Add the remaining ingredients and stir to mix well.

INTO THE OVEN Bake for 45 to 60 minutes, or until the liquid is almost completely absorbed and the top is crisp.

Makes 8 servings

Per serving: 150 calories, 6g protein, 33g carbohydrates, 1g fat, 0g saturated fat, 0mg cholesterol, 450mg sodium

Cook to Cook

WHAT ARE YOUR FAVORITE WAYS TO FLAVOR BAKED BEANS?

"I have lots of special ways to vary the flavor of a simple pot of baked beans.

Sometimes I cook up a generous amount of *hickory-smoked bacon until it's really crisp.* Then I crumble it and stir it into the beans just before serving. It makes everyone happy!

I also like to slice up franks, kielbasa, or garlic sausage and add it to the pot. I then let it simmer for about 15 minutes, so *the fabulous flavor of the sausage* gets infused into the beans. Really delicious!

If I want to *turn baked beans into a main dish,* I toss in coarsely chopped or shredded leftover chicken, turkey, or pork, along with some drained canned, diced tomatoes. I put the whole thing into a casserole and top it with some well-buttered (or oiled) freshly toasted garlicky bread crumbs. I then bake it until nice and bubbly. Oh so good!"

CHEESE & RICE SOUFFLÉ

Prep **15 MINUTES**   *Cook* **50 MINUTES**

1   **cup converted rice, uncooked**

2   **tablespoons butter or margarine**

3   **tablespoons all-purpose flour**

¾   **cup milk**

2   **cups shredded sharp Cheddar cheese (8 ounces)**

½   **teaspoon salt**

Dash of cayenne pepper

4   **large eggs, separated**

Even if you've never made a soufflé before, this one will turn out golden, high, and very impressive. It's delicious to serve with prime rib or tenderloin of beef.

LET'S BEGIN Preheat the oven to 325°F. Cook the rice according to package directions. Coat a 1½-quart casserole with cooking spray and set aside.

BUBBLE & BOIL Meanwhile, melt the butter in a medium saucepan over medium heat. Stir in the flour and cook, stirring constantly, for 1 minute. Slowly stir in the milk and cook, stirring often, for 5 minutes, or until the mixture comes to a boil and thickens. Add the cheese, salt, and cayenne and stir constantly until the cheese melts. Beat the egg yolks lightly with a fork and slowly add to the milk mixture, stirring constantly. Remove from the heat and stir in the rice.

INTO THE OVEN Place the egg whites in a large bowl and beat at high speed with an electric mixer until stiff peaks form. Gently fold the rice mixture into the egg whites. Transfer to the prepared pan and bake for 40 minutes, or until puffed and golden. Serve immediately.

Makes 5 servings

Per serving: 459 calories, 21g protein, 37g carbohydrates, 25g fat, 14g saturated fat, 233mg cholesterol, 620mg sodium

IRISH SODA BREAD

Prep **30 MINUTES**   *Cook* **1 HOUR 20 MINUTES + COOLING**

4	cups all-purpose flour
¼	cup sugar
1	tablespoon baking powder
1	teaspoon caraway seeds
1	teaspoon salt
1	teaspoon baking soda
¼	cup shortening
1½	cups raisins
1	large egg, beaten
1½	cups buttermilk
1	egg white

Don't wait for a special occasion to whip up a homey Irish soda bread. This one has the classic flavors of caraway and raisins, though some folks prefer dried currants.

LET'S BEGIN Preheat the oven to 325°F. Lightly grease a 2-quart round casserole dish and set aside. Combine the first 6 ingredients in a large mixing bowl. Cut in the shortening with a pastry blender until the mixture resembles coarse crumbs.

MAKE THE DOUGH Stir in the raisins, egg, and buttermilk and stir just until blended (the dough will be somewhat dry). Turn the dough out onto a well-floured surface and with floured hands, knead it for 8 to 10 strokes.

SHAPE & BAKE Shape the dough into a ball and place it in the prepared dish. Brush the top with the egg white and bake for 1 hour and 20 minutes, or until a toothpick inserted in the center comes out clean. (Cover the top of the bread with foil after 1 hour of baking, if necessary, to keep it from overbrowning.) Cool the bread in the dish for 10 minutes, then remove and cool completely on a wire rack.

Makes 16 servings

Per serving: 210 calories, 5g protein, 39g carbohydrates, 4g fat, 1g saturated fat, 16mg cholesterol, 110mg sodium

Food Facts

THE BACKGROUND ON IRISH SODA BREAD

Travel through Ireland and you're likely to be served Irish soda bread at almost every stop. They make it the classic way: leavened with baking soda, mixed with buttermilk, and speckled with currants or sultana raisins and caraway seeds. It's kneaded briefly on a floured board, then flattened. Before the bread goes into the oven, a cross is slashed into the top. As legend has it, the cross keeps the devil away.

Through the years, Irish soda bread was traditionally baked in a three-legged iron pot, which is connected to the saying "making pot luck" in Ireland. The pot was commonly used for baking cakes and breads, as well as for roasting and stewing. The bread was put into the pot, covered tightly, and placed near the fire to bake. Hot peat sods were placed on top to provide even heat.

SuperQuick
BUTTERMILK BISCUITS

Prep **15 MINUTES**   *Cook* **12 MINUTES**

2   cups all-purpose flour

4   teaspoons baking powder

½   teaspoon salt

½   teaspoon cream of tartar

¼   teaspoon baking soda

⅓   cup shortening

1   cup buttermilk

2   tablespoons butter or margarine, melted

Want to know the secret to the most tender and flaky biscuits? Combine the ingredients just until blended, and when cutting out the biscuits do not twist the cutter. Simply press it down and then out.

LET'S BEGIN Preheat the oven to 450°F. Combine the flour, baking powder, salt, cream of tartar, and baking soda in a large bowl and stir to mix well. Cut in the shortening using a pastry blender until the mixture resembles coarse crumbs. Add the buttermilk and stir just until the mixture forms a soft dough.

ROLL & CUT Transfer the dough to a lightly floured surface and knead 20 times, or until the dough is smooth. Pat or roll out the dough to ½-inch thickness. Cut out biscuits with a floured 2-inch cookie cutter. Gather the scraps, pat out, and cut. You should have 18 biscuits.

INTO THE OVEN Place the biscuits on an ungreased baking sheet and brush the tops with half of the butter. Bake for 12 minutes, or until golden brown. Brush with the remaining butter and serve warm.

Makes 18 servings

Per serving: 100 calories, 2g protein, 12g carbohydrates, 5g fat, 2g saturated fat, 5mg cholesterol, 220mg sodium

PESTO BREAD

Prep **15 MINUTES + RISING**   *Cook* **15 MINUTES**

1	loaf (1 pound) frozen bread dough, thawed
2	tablespoons olive oil
1	tablespoon dried pesto seasoning
¼	cup shredded Parmesan cheese

Pizza dough shaped in a pizza pan and dimpled with one's fingers is known as focaccia. But whatever you call it, it's delicious.

LET'S BEGIN Place the dough on a lightly floured surface and roll into a 12-inch circle. Transfer to a round pizza pan and cover loosely with a towel. Let the dough rise for 20 minutes.

SEASON WITH CARE Pierce the dough all over with a fork and drizzle it with the olive oil. Sprinkle with the seasoning and Parmesan. Let the dough rise 20 minutes longer. Preheat the oven to 350°F. Bake for 15 to 20 minutes, or until golden brown. Slice the bread into wedges and serve hot from the oven.

Makes 8 servings

Per serving: 193 calories, 6g protein, 29g carbohydrates, 6g fat, 1g saturated fat, 1mg cholesterol, 338mg sodium

Cooking Basics

THE SECRET TO MAKING GREAT SOUTHERN BISCUITS

During plantation days down South, baking powder had not yet been invented. One could frequently hear cooks beating the unleavened biscuit dough with a mallet or the flat side of an axe, during the morning hours.

Ask any Southern cook her secret to great biscuits. She's likely to say it's all in how you mix, handle, cut, and bake them. Here are a few tips from the best bakers we know:

• The flour: Southern cooks like to use self-rising flour, as it's low in protein and makes very tender biscuits. But don't forget to add about ⅛ teaspoon baking soda if you're using buttermilk, sour cream, or sour milk as one of the liquids.

• The fat: Many cooks use two—butter or lard and vegetable shortening. Be sure the butter is cold and cut into small pieces.

• The liquid: This varies as to how one's mother or grandmother made biscuits—with buttermilk, sour cream, sour milk, or sweet milk or cream.

• Cutting it in: Mixing the fat into the flour is one of the most important steps to light and flaky biscuits. Use two forks or a pastry blender—not your hands, as their heat will soften the butter. Cut it in until the lumps resemble good-size peas.

• Mixing it up: Stir just until the dough comes together, no more! Then let it rest 3 to 4 minutes before shaping the biscuits.

• Patting out the dough: Most cooks like to pat—not roll—out their biscuit dough, from ¾ inch to 1 inch thick.

• Shaping the biscuits: Most cooks use a round, straight-sided metal biscuit cutter, about 2 inches wide. They transfer the biscuits to a buttered cookie sheet and brush them with melted butter.

• Baking them out: Bake biscuits in a hot oven, 450°F, for 12 minutes, or until light golden brown.

SAVORY BREADSTICKS

Prep **10 MINUTES**   *Cook* **7 MINUTES**

⅓   **cup butter, melted**

½   **teaspoon paprika**

½   **teaspoon dried rosemary leaves**

¼   **teaspoon dried marjoram leaves**

¼   **teaspoon ground thyme**

⅛   **teaspoon garlic powder**

8   **partially baked soft breadsticks**

Here's how to gussy up these tasty breadsticks to serve as fabulous hors d'oeuvres. Buy thinly sliced prosciutto and wrap one slice, in a spiral, around each breadstick. Put them into a clean, low vase and serve.

LET'S BEGIN Preheat the oven to 400°F. Place the first 6 ingredients in a small bowl and stir to mix well.

INTO THE OVEN Place the breadsticks on a jelly-roll pan, brush with the butter mixture, and bake for 7 to 8 minutes, or until the breadsticks are crisp and golden brown.

Makes 8 servings

Per serving: 150 calories, 2g protein, 14g carbohydrates, 9g fat, 4g saturated fat, 20mg cholesterol, 220mg sodium

CORNBREAD

Prep **10 MINUTES**   *Cook* **35 MINUTES**

1½   cups all-purpose flour

⅔   cup sugar

½   cup yellow cornmeal

1   tablespoon baking powder

½   teaspoon salt

1¼   cups milk

2   large eggs, lightly beaten

⅓   cup vegetable oil

3   tablespoons butter or margarine, melted

This slightly sweetened cornbread is great for breakfast. It's also delicious for dessert when topped with sliced strawberries and whipped cream.

LET'S BEGIN Preheat the oven to 350°F. Grease an 8 × 8-inch baking pan and set aside.

MIX IT UP Mix the first 5 ingredients together in a medium bowl. Combine the milk, eggs, oil, and butter in a small bowl and stir to mix well. Add the milk mixture to the flour mixture and stir just until blended.

INTO THE OVEN Pour the batter into the prepared pan. Bake for 35 minutes, or until a toothpick inserted in the center comes out clean.

> **Makes 12 servings**
>
> *Per serving: 228 calories, 4g protein, 30g carbohydrates, 11g fat, 3g saturated fat, 46mg cholesterol, 201mg sodium*

CORN MUFFINS

Spoon the batter into 18 to 20 greased or paper-lined muffin cups, filling two-thirds full. Bake for 18 to 20 minutes, or until a toothpick inserted in the centers comes out clean. Cool in pans on wire racks for 5 minutes. Serve warm.

Banana Apple Betty, page 126

Dish Up Dessert!

At least as far back as the mid-19th century, folks have been dishing up fruit cobblers, crisps, slumps, bread puddings, and Betties to serve at suppertime all across America. In those days, these homey desserts were not meant for company, but today many have gone upscale with a splash of liqueur, exotic combinations of fruits, or flavored whipped cream. Other desserts have been coming out of ovens for centuries, too, such as homemade fruit pies, overstuffed baked apples, and gingerbread. We just couldn't create a book on easy dishes from the oven without including some of these tried-and-true (and scrumptious!) favorites. So here they are. Take a minute to read some food facts about a few of them, then pick out your favorite and make it for supper tonight.

KIWIFRUIT COBBLER

Prep **20 MINUTES**   *Bake* **43 MINUTES**

12	large kiwifruit, peeled and cut into ¾-inch cubes
3	tablespoons firmly packed brown sugar
1	tablespoon grated lemon zest
1	tablespoon all-purpose flour
½	teaspoon ground cinnamon
½	package (3.2 ounces) corn muffin mix
½	teaspoon ground nutmeg

Vanilla ice cream or whipped cream (optional)

It isn't often that kiwifruit is used in a baked dessert, but this is an easy and great-tasting treat. When measuring the brown sugar, be sure to pack it into the tablespoon.

LET'S BEGIN Preheat the oven to 375°F. Coat a 2-quart baking dish with cooking spray and place the kiwifruit in the dish.

INTO THE OVEN Combine 2 tablespoons of the brown sugar, the lemon zest, flour, and cinnamon in a small bowl and stir to mix well. Add the mixture to the baking dish and toss lightly to combine with the kiwi. Bake for 25 minutes.

TOP IT OFF Meanwhile, prepare the half package of muffin mix according to package directions. Remove the kiwi dish from the oven and spoon the prepared mix over it. Sprinkle the nutmeg and the remaining sugar over the top and bake 18 to 20 minutes longer, or until the top is golden brown. Serve warm, with ice cream or whipped cream, if you wish.

Makes 6 servings

Per serving: 210 calories, 3g protein, 48g carbohydrates, 3g fat, 1g saturated fat, 5mg cholesterol, 160mg sodium

SuperQuick
CHERRY PEACH COBBLER

Prep **10 MINUTES**   *Bake* **18 MINUTES**

1	can (21 ounces) cherry fruit filling
1	can (21 ounces) peach fruit filling
⅓	cup sugar
½	teaspoon ground cinnamon
1	can (10 ounces) refrigerated flaky biscuits
4	tablespoons butter or margarine, melted

Flavorful cherry and peach fruit fillings make this recipe a snap to put together. Dipping the biscuits into melted butter does two things: It gives them extra rich flavor and makes it easy for the cinnamon and sugar to cling.

LET'S BEGIN Preheat the oven to 400°F. Combine the cherry and peach fillings in a 13 × 9-inch baking dish. Combine the sugar and cinnamon in a small bowl and stir to mix well.

TOP IT OFF Pull apart each biscuit into two rounds. Dip each dough round into the butter and then into the cinnamon sugar. Arrange on top of the filling.

INTO THE OVEN Bake for 18 to 20 minutes, or until the biscuits are golden brown. Serve the cobbler warm.

Makes 8 servings

Per serving: 350 calories, 4g protein, 59g carbohydrates, 11g fat, 4g saturated fat, 16mg cholesterol, 390mg sodium

Time Savers

CUTTING PREP TIME WHEN MAKING COBBLERS

Cobbler, a deep-dish fruit filling topped with biscuits, is as all-American as apple pie.

But the truth is, putting together the filling and topping takes time, so here are some super-fast ways to get this dessert treat on your dinner table without a lot of work.

For the filling—instead of fresh fruit, use drained pie filling, pie filling with some fresh berries added (no work there!), or drained canned fruit (peaches, apricots, or pears) with raisins tossed in.

For the topping—use refrigerated biscuits, unrolled crescent roll dough sprinkled with cinnamon and sugar, or buttermilk baking mix biscuits.

BREAD PUDDING WITH RUM RAISIN SAUCE

Prep **20 MINUTES + STANDING**   *Bake* **45 MINUTES**

4   cups stale cake doughnuts (about 5), cut into 1-inch pieces

4   cups stale bread, cut into 1-inch pieces

¼   cup butter or margarine, melted

1   cup milk

1   cup heavy cream

4   large eggs

1   cup sugar

2   teaspoons pumpkin pie spice

Rum Raisin Sauce (see recipe)

What a clever way to use stale cake doughnuts. Instead of cutting the doughnuts into one-inch pieces, it may be just as easy to break them into chunks.

LET'S BEGIN Coat a 2-quart baking dish with cooking spray and set aside. Place the doughnuts and bread in the baking dish.

WHISK & REST Put the butter, milk, cream, eggs, sugar, and pumpkin pie spice in a large bowl and whisk to mix well. Pour the mixture over the doughnuts and bread and let stand for 15 minutes. (At this point, the mixture can be covered and refrigerated for up to 24 hours before baking.)

INTO THE OVEN Preheat the oven to 350°F. Bake for 45 minutes, or until the center is set. Serve with the Rum Raisin Sauce.

RUM RAISIN SAUCE

Combine ½ cup water, ½ cup sugar, 2 tablespoons butter, ¼ cup spiced rum, and ½ cup raisins in a medium saucepan. Bring the mixture to a boil over medium-high heat. Stir in ¼ cup heavy cream, reduce the heat, and simmer for 10 minutes, stirring occasionally. Pour the rum sauce over the warm bread pudding.

Makes 12 servings
Per serving: 417 calories, 5g protein, 48g carbohydrates, 22g fat, 11g saturated fat, 129mg cholesterol, 257mg sodium

BRANDIED CHERRY CHOCOLATE BREAD PUDDING WITH VANILLA SAUCE

Prep **20 MINUTES + STANDING**   *Bake* **45 MINUTES**

1   cup dried cherries

½   cup brandy

4   cups stale cake doughnuts (about 5), cut into 1-inch pieces

4   cups stale bagels (about 3), cut into 1-inch pieces

4   large eggs

2   cups heavy cream

1   cup light cream

2   teaspoons ground cinnamon

½   teaspoon chili powder

1   tablespoon vanilla extract

¾   cup firmly packed brown sugar

¼   cup Dutch processed cocoa

¼   teaspoon salt

¾   cup chopped pecans

4   ounces bittersweet baking chocolate, chopped (¾ cup)

Vanilla Sauce (see recipe)

Don't think twice about adding the small amount of chili powder to the cocoa mixture. It just adds an intriguing touch of rich flavor. In fact, it is a very Mexican thing to do.

LET'S BEGIN Combine the cherries and the brandy in a small bowl and let stand to soak for 30 to 60 minutes. Coat a 13 × 9-inch baking pan with cooking spray. Place the doughnuts and bagels in the pan.

WHISK & REST Combine the eggs, heavy cream, light cream, cinnamon, chili powder, vanilla, sugar, cocoa, and salt in a large bowl and whisk to mix well. Stir in the pecans, chocolate, and cherry-brandy mixture. Pour over the doughnuts and bagels and let stand for 15 minutes. (At this point the mixture can be covered and refrigerated for up to 24 hours before baking.)

INTO THE OVEN Preheat the oven to 350°F. Bake for 45 to 55 minutes, or until the center of the pudding is set. Serve with the Vanilla Sauce.

VANILLA SAUCE

Combine 1 cup sugar, 1 tablespoon all-purpose flour, ½ cup light cream, and ½ cup butter in a medium saucepan. Bring the mixture to a boil over medium-high heat, stirring constantly, for 2 minutes or until slightly thickened. Stir in 1 tablespoon vanilla extract. Serve the sauce with the bread pudding.

Makes 12 servings
Per serving: 678 calories, 9g protein, 71g carbohydrates, 39g fat, 19g saturated fat, 163mg cholesterol, 344mg sodium

BANANA APPLE BETTY

Prep **20 MINUTES**   *Bake* **30 MINUTES**

2   cups soft bread crumbs

½   cup firmly packed brown sugar

⅓   cup granulated sugar

½   teaspoon ground cinnamon

2   large firm bananas, sliced

2   Granny Smith apples, cored and cut into chunks

¼   cup orange juice

⅛   teaspoon ground nutmeg

3   tablespoons butter or margarine, cut into small pieces

Frozen whipped topping, thawed (optional)

Cozy fruit desserts that are topped with fresh bread crumbs are commonly known as betties. We love using Granny Smith apples for their rich tart flavor and for their assured availability.

LET'S BEGIN Preheat the oven to 375°F. Coat a 9-inch cake pan with cooking spray and set aside. Combine the bread crumbs, brown sugar, granulated sugar, and ¼ teaspoon of the cinnamon in a medium bowl and stir to mix well. Set aside. Combine the bananas, apples, orange juice, nutmeg, and the remaining ¼ teaspoon cinnamon in a medium bowl and toss to coat.

LAYER Sprinkle 2 tablespoons of the crumb mixture into the prepared pan. Spread the fruit mixture over the crumbs. Dot the fruit with the butter and sprinkle the remaining crumb mixture over the fruit.

INTO THE OVEN Bake for 30 to 35 minutes, or until the apples are tender. Cool slightly before serving. Serve with whipped topping, if you wish.

Makes 8 servings
Per serving: 277 calories, 4g protein, 54g carbohydrates, 6g fat, 1g saturated fat, 12mg cholesterol, 288mg sodium

Food Facts

THE PAST OF BROWN BETTY

Though betties appear to have been baked since colonial times in America, they didn't show up in cookbooks until the 1800s. In fact, Fannie Farmer does not include one in her historic 1896 cookbook, *The Boston Cooking-School Cook Book*. But she does include a recipe for scalloped apples, which is fairly identical to a classic betty. By the 1930 edition of her cookbook, a recipe for Brown Betty does appear.

Betties seem to have been created as the ideal way to use up leftover bread. But leftover sponge cake, pound cake, and angel food cake can and have been used with great success. They can be made with many different fruits, but the one called Apple Brown Betty is the most famous. It is made by alternating layers of sugared and spiced apples with buttered bread crumbs. Then it is drizzled with a little fruit juice and baked until browned and crisp on top.

Piña Colada Bread Pudding

Prep **15 minutes** *Bake* **40 minutes**

1   can (20 ounces) pineapple tidbits

6   cups dry raisin bread cubes

1½   cups milk

1   cup liquid piña colada mix

¾   cup sugar

½   cup chopped pecans

3   large eggs, beaten

1   cup heavy cream

2   tablespoons dark rum

It's hard to get enough of the taste of piña coladas, so here is a creative way to get your fix. Be sure to use dark, not light, rum here.

LET'S BEGIN Preheat the oven to 350°F. Coat a 13 × 9-inch baking dish with cooking spray and set aside. Drain the pineapple, reserving ½ cup of the juice to make the topping.

MIX IT UP Place the bread cubes in a large bowl. Add the milk and the piña colada mix, stir to combine, and let stand for 5 minutes. Stir again, crushing the bread cubes with a large spoon. Add the sugar, pecans, eggs, and pineapple and stir to combine.

INTO THE OVEN Pour the mixture into the prepared dish and bake for 40 to 45 minutes, or until firm and lightly browned. Meanwhile, combine the cream, rum, and the reserved pineapple juice in a large bowl. Whisk together until slightly thickened. Serve with the warm bread pudding.

Makes 12 servings

Per serving: 341 calories, 6g protein, 48g carbohydrates, 14g fat, 6g saturated fat, 83mg cholesterol, 159mg sodium

---

Food Facts

BREAD 'N' BUTTER PUDDINGS

Its definition belies the true treat that this is: a simple and delicious baked dessert made with cubes or slices of bread that are saturated with a custard mixture.

Historically, bread puddings are an English invention, enjoyed hot, warm, or cold by all manner of folks. Some bread puddings earned fancy names, such as Summer Pudding and Queen's Pudding, while others are simply named

Bread and Butter Pudding.

Clever cooks have embraced bread pudding as a way to use up especially tasty forms of bread, including brioche, panettone, challah, raisin bread, and even cake. Almost every cuisine has enjoyed some form of bread pudding. The Egyptians have a dessert called *Om Ali* that is made with phyllo dough, raisins, milk, and almonds. A Middle Eastern dessert called *Eish es Serny* ("pal-

ace bread") is made by drying slices of bread to form rusks, which are then simmered in honey and sugar syrup. In India there is a dessert called *Shahi Tukra*, which is made with fried bread that is dipped into a rose water and saffron syrup and then covered with a creamy sauce and almonds.

It is clear that simple bread puddings have been embraced worldwide and have become a universal sweet treat enjoyed by all.

CARIBBEAN BANANA CAKE

Prep **15 MINUTES** *Bake* **30 MINUTES**

2	cups all-purpose flour
2	teaspoons baking powder
1	teaspoon baking soda
½	teaspoon ground cinnamon
½	teaspoon ground nutmeg
½	cup butter or margarine, softened
1½	cups sugar
2	large eggs
3	ripe medium bananas, mashed (about 1 cup)
¾	cup low-fat milk
1	container (16 ounces) prepared coconut-pecan frosting

This fabulous cake contains some of the tasty sweet flavors of the Caribbean: banana, coconut, and pecans. To save on cleanup, line the baking pan with heavy-duty foil and then coat it with nonstick spray.

LET'S BEGIN Preheat the oven to 350°F. Coat a 13 × 9-inch baking pan with cooking spray and set aside. Mix the first 5 ingredients together in a medium bowl. Set aside.

MIX IT UP Combine the butter and sugar in a large bowl and beat at medium speed with an electric mixer until creamy. Beat in the eggs and bananas. Alternately beat in one-third of the milk and one-half of the flour mixture, ending with the milk.

INTO THE OVEN Pour the batter into the prepared pan and bake for 30 to 35 minutes, or until a toothpick inserted in the center comes out clean. Cool the cake completely on a wire rack. Spread the frosting over the cooled cake.

Makes 12 servings

Per serving: 452 calories, 6g protein, 67g carbohydrates, 19g fat, 5g saturated fat, 72mg cholesterol, 306mg sodium

UPSIDE-DOWN CAKE

Prep **15 MINUTES**   *Bake* **40 MINUTES**

1   **can (20 ounces) pineapple slices**

¼   **cup butter or margarine, melted**

⅔   **cup firmly packed brown sugar**

10   **maraschino cherries**

1   **package (18¼ ounces) pineapple-flavored or yellow cake mix**

Pineapple upside-down cake is a time-honored American dessert. Canned pineapple and pineapple-flavored cake mix make this rendition easy as well as tasty. Traditionally, a cast-iron skillet was used to bake this cake. If you have one, use it.

LET'S BEGIN Preheat the oven to 350°F. Drain the pineapple, reserving ¾ cup of the juice. Combine the butter and sugar in a 12-inch ovenproof skillet and stir to mix well. Arrange the pineapple slices on top of the sugar mixture. Place a cherry in the center of each pineapple slice.

MIX IT UP Prepare the cake mix according to the package directions, replacing the water with the reserved ¾ cup pineapple juice. Pour the batter evenly over the pineapple slices.

INTO THE OVEN Bake for 40 to 45 minutes, or until a toothpick inserted in the center comes out clean. Cool the cake for 5 minutes. Loosen the edges by running a knife between the cake and the sides of the pan. Invert onto a serving platter.

> *Makes 10 servings*
>
> *Per serving: 430 calories, 4g protein, 67g carbohydrates, 17g fat, 5g saturated fat, 79g cholesterol, 393mg sodium*

RECTANGULAR CAKE

If you wish, you may bake this cake in a 13 × 9-inch baking pan instead of a skillet. Prepare and assemble the cake as directed above, except cut two pineapple slices in half, then place the whole slices along the edges of the pan and the halved slices in the center. Place cherries in the center of the slices. Bake and cool as above.

SUGAR LEMON SQUARES

Prep **15 MINUTES**   *Bake* **27 MINUTES**

CRUST

¾   cup all-purpose flour

½   cup confectioners' sugar

½   cup reduced fat butter,
     cut into small pieces

FILLING

1   large egg

1   egg white

1   cup granulated sugar

2   tablespoons grated
     lemon zest

2   tablespoons all-purpose
     flour

6   tablespoons lemon juice

1   drop yellow food
     coloring (optional)

⅓   cup confectioners' sugar

Lemon squares are always a treat. They are delicious as is, or they can be dressed up with whipped cream and fresh raspberries.

LET'S BEGIN Preheat the oven to 375°F. Coat an 8 × 8-inch glass baking dish with cooking spray. To make the crust, mix all ingredients together in a medium bowl and stir until the mixture forms a sticky dough. Place the dough in the prepared pan and top with plastic wrap. Using your fingers against the plastic, press the dough onto the bottom and 1 inch up the sides of the baking dish. Remove the plastic and bake for 12 to 14 minutes, or until the edges are light brown.

BEAT IT Meanwhile, make the filling. Combine the first 4 ingredients in a medium bowl. Beat at medium speed with an electric mixer until light and fluffy. Stir in the flour, lemon juice, and food coloring, if you wish. Pour the mixture over the crust.

INTO THE OVEN Bake 15 minutes longer, or until the filling is set. Cool completely, then cut into 25 bars. Sprinkle the bars with sifted confectioners' sugar.

Makes 25 bars

Per bar: 76 calories, 1g protein, 14g carbohydrates, 2g fat, 1g saturated fat, 15mg cholesterol, 34mg sodium

Very Cherry Pie

Prep **30 MINUTES** *Bake* **1 HOUR**

Pastry for a double-crust pie

4   cups frozen unsweetened tart cherries (do not thaw), or 2 cans unsweetened pie cherries (16 ounces each), well drained

1   cup dried tart cherries

1   cup sugar

2   tablespoons quick-cooking tapioca

½   teaspoon almond extract

¼   teaspoon ground nutmeg

1   tablespoon butter, cut into pieces

Enjoy a fabulous cherry pie without a lot of work: All it takes is cherry pie filling and flaky refrigerated piecrusts. Don't even think of leaving out the almond extract. Even a half teaspoon adds rich flavor.

LET'S BEGIN Preheat the oven to 375°F. On a lightly floured surface, roll half the pastry into a ⅛-inch-thick round. Fold in half and ease gently into a 9-inch pie pan. Unfold the dough, letting the pastry overhang the edge. Trim the pastry to 1 inch from the rim of the pan. Refrigerate while making the filling.

FILLING Combine the frozen cherries, dried cherries, sugar, tapioca, and almond extract in a large bowl and mix well. Let the filling stand at room temperature for 15 minutes. Spoon the filling into the pie shell and sprinkle with the nutmeg. Dot with the butter. Roll the remaining pastry into a ⅛-inch-thick round and cut into ½-inch strips. Use to weave a lattice top by arranging strips on the pie at 1-inch intervals. Fold back alternate strips to weave crosswise strips over and under. Seal and flute the edge.

INTO THE OVEN Bake for 1 hour, or until the crust is golden brown and the filling is bubbly. (If necessary, cover the edge of the crust with foil during baking to prevent overbrowning.) Cool completely on a wire rack.

Makes 8 servings

Per serving: 448 calories, 4g protein, 73g carbohydrates, 17g total fat, 5g saturated fat, 4mg cholesterol, 265mg sodium

STUFFED BAKED APPLES

Prep **20 MINUTES**   *Bake* **30 MINUTES**

6   small baking apples (Rome, Golden Delicious, Winesap, or Imperial)

½   cup rolled oats

⅓   cup crushed graham crackers

4   tablespoons firmly packed brown sugar

1   tablespoon sliced almonds

1   tablespoon butter or margarine, softened

1   teaspoon lemon juice

¼   teaspoon ground cinnamon

1   cup warm water

1   tablespoon granulated sugar

Stuffed baked apples are homey and are tasty served hot, cold, or at room temperature. For breakfast, a generous dollop of vanilla yogurt makes them a real morning treat.

LET'S BEGIN Preheat the oven to 350°F. Starting at the top of each apple, core them to ½ inch above the bottom. Use a knife or potato peeler to hollow out the inside of the apple, leaving a 1-inch shell around the edges. Reserve the centers of the apples and chop them into small pieces.

STUFF 'EM Combine ⅔ cup of the chopped apple with the oats, graham crackers, 3½ tablespoons of the brown sugar, the almonds, butter, lemon juice, and cinnamon in a medium bowl and stir to mix well. Stand the cored apples in an 8-inch baking pan. Fill the apples with the oat mixture and sprinkle the tops with the remaining brown sugar.

INTO THE OVEN Combine the water and the granulated sugar in a small bowl and stir until the sugar melts. Pour into the baking pan around, not over, the apples. Bake the apples for 30 to 40 minutes, or until tender but not mushy.

Makes 6 apples

Per apple: 168 calories, 2g protein, 36g carbohydrates, 3g fat, 1g saturated fat, 5mg cholesterol, 42mg sodium

Cook to Cook

WHAT ARE SOME THINGS I CAN STUFF INTO AN APPLE?

Apples are such wonderfully versatile fruit. Depending on my mood, here are a few of my very favorites:

When I want something simple and delicious, I stuff each apple with *a nice pat of butter,* then fill each cavity with pure maple syrup.

I sometimes make a mix of *my favorite granola,* ground cinnamon, and melted butter and use it to stuff apples.

My favorite stuffing is a combination of finely *chopped dried fruits* to which I add chopped nuts. I moisten it with apricot nectar (or brandy) and melted butter. I serve the apples with soft whipped cream. Boy is that ever good!

LEMON CURD TARTLETS

Prep **15 MINUTES + CHILLING**   *Cook* **20 MINUTES**

TART SHELLS

1   cup all-purpose flour

½   cup confectioners' sugar

½   teaspoon salt

½   cup unsalted butter, chilled and cut into pieces

1   egg yolk

2   tablespoons cold water

1   teaspoon fresh-squeezed lemon juice

FILLING

2   tablespoons grated lemon zest

1   cup fresh-squeezed lemon juice

1⅓ cups granulated sugar

4   large eggs

Pinch of salt

½   cup + 6 tablespoons unsalted butter, cut into pieces

Whipped cream or confectioners' sugar (optional)

Once you see how easy it is to make lemon curd from scratch, you will definitely want to make an extra batch of it. Spoon it over toast for a fabulous breakfast or serve it alongside muffins, biscuits, or scones. So delicious!

LET'S BEGIN Preheat the oven to 350°F. To make the crust, measure the flour, confectioners' sugar, and salt into a food processor and pulse to combine. Add the butter and pulse until the mixture resembles coarse meal. Place the egg yolk, water, and lemon juice in a small bowl and whisk to combine. Add to the food processor and pulse until pea-size lumps form and the dough holds together when squeezed (dough will appear somewhat crumbly).

SHAPE & BAKE Press a small amount of dough (a ball the diameter of a nickel) evenly into the bottom of 18 miniature muffin pan cups and refrigerate for 20 minutes. Using your thumb and forefinger, spread the dough evenly on the bottom and around the sides of each muffin cup. Place the muffin pans on a baking pan and bake for 12 to 15 minutes, or until golden brown. Let cool slightly, remove the crusts from the pans, and cool completely.

COOK & STIR Meanwhile, make the filling. Combine the lemon zest and juice, granulated sugar, eggs, and salt in a medium heavy-bottomed saucepan and whisk to mix well. Add the butter and cook over low heat, whisking constantly, for 8 to 10 minutes, or until the mixture thickens. Pour through a fine wire mesh sieve into a bowl, cover, and cool to room temperature. Chill the mixture. Just before serving, spoon into the prepared shells and garnish with whipped cream or a dusting of confectioners' sugar, if you wish.

Makes 18 tartlets
Per tartlet: 250 calories, 2g protein, 24g carbohydrates, 16g fat, 10g saturated fat, 98mg cholesterol, 99mg sodium

BANANA GINGERBREAD BARS

Prep **15 MINUTES**   *Bake* **20 MINUTES**

1   very ripe medium
     banana + 1 small banana

1   package (14½ ounces)
     gingerbread cake mix

½   cup lukewarm water

1   large egg

½   cup raisins

½   cup slivered almonds

1½   cups confectioners'
     sugar + additional for
     sprinkling (optional)

3   tablespoons lemon juice

There's something wonderful and loving about the aroma of ginger-bread baking in the oven. If you like, you can use dried tart cherries or dried cranberries in place of the raisins. And as much as the almonds are pretty perfect here, pecans or walnuts will also work well.

LET'S BEGIN Preheat the oven to 350°F. Coat a 13 × 9-inch baking pan with cooking spray and set aside. Cut the medium banana into slices and puree in a blender to measure ½ cup banana puree.

MIX IT UP Combine the gingerbread mix, water, egg, and banana puree in a large bowl. Beat on low speed with an electric mixer for 1 minute. Chop the small banana (about ½ cup) and stir into the batter. Add the raisins and almonds and stir to combine.

INTO THE OVEN Spread the batter into the prepared pan. Bake for 20 to 25 minutes, or until the center is springy to the touch. Combine the sugar and lemon juice in a medium bowl and stir to combine. Spread the glaze over the warm gingerbread. Cool before cutting into bars. Sprinkle with the extra confectioners' sugar, if you wish.

Makes 32 bars

Per bar: 106 calories, 1g protein, 19g carbohydrates, 3g fat, 1g saturated fat, 7mg cholesterol, 87mg sodium

CHOCOLATE SPONGE CUSTARD

Prep **15 MINUTES**   *Bake* **30 MINUTES**

3   large eggs, separated

¼   teaspoon cream of tartar

1¼   cups milk

⅓   cup chocolate-flavored syrup

¼   cup all-purpose flour

¾   teaspoon vanilla extract

Marshmallow fluff or whipped cream (optional)

Did you know that eggs are easiest to separate when cold from the refrigerator. Tips like these guarantee you success when you whip up this special dessert.

LET'S BEGIN Preheat the oven to 350°F. Coat 6 custard cups (6 ounces each) with cooking spray and set aside. Combine the egg whites and cream of tartar in a large mixing bowl and beat at high speed with an electric mixer until stiff peaks form. Set aside.

MIX IT UP Combine the egg yolks, milk, syrup, flour, and vanilla in a medium bowl and beat at medium speed with an electric mixer until smooth. Fold the milk mixture into the beaten egg whites.

INTO THE OVEN Pour the mixture evenly into the prepared cups and place the cups in a large, deep baking pan. Place the pan into the oven and pour hot water in the pan to within ½ inch of the top of the cups. Bake for 30 to 35 minutes, or until puffed and a toothpick inserted in the centers comes out clean. Remove from the water and cool for 5 minutes before serving. Serve with marshmallow fluff or whipped cream, if you wish.

Makes 6 servings

Per serving: 134 calories, 6g protein, 17g carbohydrates, 4g fat, 2g saturated fat, 111mg cholesterol, 69mg sodium

APPLE SUNFLOWER STRUDEL

Prep **20 MINUTES + STANDING**   *Bake* **45 MINUTES**

1²⁄₃ cups all-purpose flour

¼ teaspoon salt

2 tablespoons sunflower oil

1 tablespoon vinegar

1 large egg, lightly beaten

¼ cup warm water

¼ cup granulated sugar

½ cup firmly packed brown sugar

2 tablespoons cornstarch

1½ teaspoons ground cinnamon

5½ cups chopped tart apples

1½ tablespoons lemon juice

½ cup + 2 tablespoons raw sunflower kernels

2 tablespoons + 1 teaspoon butter, softened

2 teaspoons honey

Vanilla ice cream (optional)

If you have never attempted to make strudel dough from scratch, this is your chance! You will be truly surprised at how easy it is. The addition of vinegar to the dough is an old-fashioned trick: It ensures that the dough will be nice and tender.

LET'S BEGIN Combine the flour, salt, oil, vinegar, and egg in a medium bowl and stir to mix well. Stir in the water until a soft dough forms. Transfer to a lightly floured surface and knead the dough until it is smooth. Place in a bowl, cover, and set aside for 1 hour.

SEASON & SPICE Preheat the oven to 400°F. Coat a cookie sheet with cooking spray and set aside. Combine the granulated and brown sugars, the cornstarch, and cinnamon in a small bowl and stir to mix well. Set aside. Lightly flour a pastry cloth (or clean kitchen towel), place the dough on the cloth, and roll into a 12 × 8-inch rectangle. Spread the apples over the dough and sprinkle with the lemon juice. Sprinkle with the sugar mixture and ½ cup of the sunflower kernels. Dot with 2 tablespoons of the butter.

ROLL & BAKE Use the pastry cloth to lift the dough and roll it up lengthwise, jelly-roll fashion, into a cylinder. Pinch the edges together to seal. Place the strudel on the cookie sheet and bake for 35 minutes. Combine the honey and the remaining 1 teaspoon butter in a small bowl and stir to mix well. Remove the strudel from the oven, brush with the honey mixture, and sprinkle with the remaining 2 tablespoons sunflower kernels. Bake 10 minutes longer. Slice and serve with vanilla ice cream, if you wish.

Makes 8 servings
Per serving: 375 calories, 6g protein, 60g carbohydrates, 14g fat, 3g saturated fat, 36mg cholesterol, 114mg sodium

Autumn Pumpkin Soufflé

Prep **20 MINUTES**   *Bake* **15 MINUTES**

Sugar for dusting + ½ cup
   sugar

6   large eggs, separated

¾   teaspoon cream of tartar

½   cup canned solid-pack
     pumpkin

½   teaspoon pumpkin pie
     spice

Crushed gingersnaps
   (optional)

Welcome autumn with this easy and delicious hot soufflé. To guarantee success, be sure to whip the egg whites just until stiff peaks form.

LET'S BEGIN Preheat the oven to 375°F. Coat 4 soufflé dishes (8 ounces each) with cooking spray and dust lightly with sugar. Set aside. Place the egg whites and cream of tartar in a large bowl and beat at high speed with an electric mixer until foamy. Add the remaining ½ cup sugar, 2 tablespoons at a time, beating constantly, until the sugar is dissolved and stiff peaks form. Set aside.

MIX IT UP Place the egg yolks in a medium bowl and beat at medium speed with an electric mixer until thick and lemon-colored. Add the pumpkin and the spice and stir to mix well. Gently fold the pumpkin mixture into the beaten egg whites.

INTO THE OVEN Spoon the mixture evenly into the prepared dishes and place the dishes in a deep baking pan. Place the pan in the oven and pour hot water in the pan to within ½ inch of the top of the dishes. Bake for 15 to 20 minutes, or until puffy and lightly browned. Top with crushed gingersnaps, if you wish. Serve immediately.

Makes 4 servings

Per serving: 235 calories, 10g protein, 32g carbohydrates, 8g fat, 2g saturated fat, 317mg cholesterol, 107mg sodium

CREDITS

PAGE 2 National Pork Board: Photo for Caribbean Roast Pork courtesy of the National Pork Board. Used with permission.

PAGE 8 Sargento: Photo for Snapper Veracruz courtesy of Sargento Foods Inc. Used with permission.

PAGE 16 Sargento: Photo for Mom's Mac & Cheese courtesy of Sargento Foods Inc. Used with permission.

PAGE 18 Sargento: Photo and recipe for Classic Lasagna courtesy of the Sargento Foods, Inc. Used with permission.

PAGE 19 Sargento: Photo and recipe for Italian Sausage & Pasta Bake courtesy of Sargento Foods, Inc. Used with permission.

PAGE 20 Sargento: Recipe for 3-Cheese Manicotti courtesy of Sargento Foods, Inc. Used with permission.

PAGE 21 Del Monte: Recipe for Ravioli Bake courtesy of Del Monte Foods. Used with permission.

PAGE 22 National Pasta Association: Recipe for Zesty Ziti Bake courtesy of the National Pasta Association. Used with permission.

PAGE 23 B&G Foods: Recipe for Beef Nacho Casserole courtesy of B&G Foods. Used with permission.

PAGES 24/25 Mrs. T's Pierogies: Photo and recipe for Mediterranean Pierogies courtesy of Mrs. T's Pierogies. Used with permission.

PAGE 28 Birds Eye Foods: Recipe for Hobo Casserole courtesy of Birds Eye Foods. Used with permission.

PAGE 29 Wisconsin Milk Marketing Board: Recipe for Cheesy Ham & Noodle Casserole courtesy of the Wisconsin Milk Marketing Board, Inc. Used with permission.

PAGES 28/29 Nestlé: Photo and recipe for Cornbread & Beef Casserole courtesy of Nestlé. All trademarks are owned by Société des Produits Nestlé S.A., Vevey, Switzerland. Used with permission.

PAGE 30 Bumble Bee: Recipe for Classic Tuna Noodle Casserole courtesy of Bumble bee Seafoods. Used with permission.

PAGE 31 Sargento: Recipe for Mom's Mac & Cheese courtesy of Sargento Foods, Inc. Used with permission.

PAGE 32 National Pork Board: Photo for Stuffed Pork Chops courtesy of the National Pork Board. Used with permission.

PAGE 34 French's: Recipe for Smokin' Calypso Brisket courtesy of Frank's® RedHot® Cayenne Pepper Sauce. Used with permission.

PAGE 35 Cattlemen's Beef Board: Photo and recipe for Winter BBQ Beef Short Ribs courtesy of Cattlemen's Beef Board and National Cattlemen's Beef Association. Used with permission.

PAGES 36/37 Land O'Lakes: Photo and recipe for Prime Rib with Vegetable Yorkshire Pudding courtesy of Land O'Lakes, Inc. Used with permission.

PAGES 38 Land O'Lakes: Photo and recipe for Corned Beef & Cabbage courtesy of Land O'Lakes, Inc. Used with permission.

PAGE 39 Uncle Ben's: Recipe for Beef & Broccoli Au Gratin courtesy of UNCLE BEN'S® Brand. Used with permission.

PAGE 40 Quaker: Recipe for Sunday Supper Meat Loaf with Roasted Vegetables courtesy of The Quaker Oats Company. Used with permission.

PAGE 41 Cattlemen's Beef Board: Recipe for Roast Beef Cheddar Pockets courtesy of Cattlemen's Beef Board and National Cattlemen's Beef Association. Used with permission.

PAGES 42/43 Cattlemen's Beef Board: Photo and recipe for Beef-Stuffed Peppers courtesy of Cattlemen's Beef Board and National Cattlemen's Beef Association. Used with permission.

PAGE 44 National Honey Board: Recipe for Honey-Glazed Rack of Lamb courtesy of the National Honey Board. Used with permission.

PAGE 45 National Pork Board: Recipe for Apricot-Glazed Ham courtesy of the National Pork Board. Used with permission.

PAGES 46/47 National Pork Board: Recipe for Caribbean Roast Pork courtesy of the National Pork Board. Used with permission.

PAGE 48 National Pork Board: Recipe for Peppered Pork Pot Roast courtesy of the National Pork Board. Used with permission.

PAGE 49 Ocean Spray Cranberries: Photo and recipe for Spicy Cranberry Pork Chops courtesy of Ocean Spray Cranberries, Inc. Used with permission.

PAGES 50/51 National Pork Board: Photo and recipe for Stuffed Pork Chops courtesy of the National Pork Board. Used with permission.

PAGE 52 National Honey Board: Recipe for Honey-Glazed Spareribs courtesy of the National Honey Board. Used with permission.

PAGE 53 National Pork Board: Recipe for Sausage & Rice Bake courtesy of the National Pork Board. Used with permission.

PAGE 53 Del Monte: Recipe for Beef Casserole Italiano courtesy of Del Monte Foods. Used with permission.

PAGES 54/55 National Pork Board: Recipe for Crispy Mandarin Riblets courtesy of the National Pork Board. Used with permission.

PAGE 56 American Egg Board: Photo and recipe for Country Quiche courtesy of the American Egg Board. Used with permission.

PAGE 57 Birds Eye Foods: Recipe for Never-Fail Cheese Soufflé courtesy of Birds Eye Foods. Used with permission.

PAGE 58 Sargento: Photo and recipe for Bacon Cheddar Cheese Puffs courtesy of Sargento Foods Inc. Used with permission.

PAGE 59 Dole: Photo and recipe for Mini Pineapple Bacon Galettes courtesy

of Dole Food Company. Used with permission.

PAGE 60 Sargento: Photo for Chicken Cordon Bleu courtesy of Sargento Foods Inc. Used with permission.

PAGE 62 Land O'Lakes: Recipe for Herb Butter Roasted Chicken courtesy of Land O'Lakes, Inc. Used with permission.

PAGE 63 Sunkist: Recipe for Crispy Lemon Chicken courtesy of Sunkist Growers, Inc. Used with permission.

PAGE 63 National Chicken Council: Recipe for Southern Pecan Crusted Chicken courtesy of the National Chicken Council/U.S. Egg & Poultry Association. Used with permission.

PAGE 64 National Chicken Council: Recipe for Roasted Chicken with Winter Vegetable Stuffing courtesy of the National Chicken Council/U.S. Egg & Poultry Association. Used with permission.

PAGE 65 National Chicken Council: Recipe for Dill Chicken in Foil courtesy of the National Chicken Council/U.S. Egg & Poultry Association. Used with permission.

PAGES 66/67 Dole: Photo and recipe for Baked Chicken with Mandarin Sauce courtesy of Dole Food Company. Used with permission.

PAGE 68 National Honey Board: Recipe for Oven-Fried Honey Chicken courtesy of the National Honey Board. Used with permission.

PAGE 69 Sargento: Recipe for Chicken Cordon Bleu courtesy of Sargento Foods Inc. Used with permission.

PAGE 70 Del Monte: Recipe for Chicken Parmesan courtesy of Del Monte Foods. Used with permission.

PAGE 71 Zatarain's: Recipe for Creole Chicken courtesy of Zatarain's. Used with permission.

PAGE 72 Bruce Foods: Recipe for Crispy Herb-Topped Chicken courtesy of Bruce Foods Corporation. Used with permission.

PAGE 72 Birds Eye Foods: Recipe for Vegetable, Chicken & Rice Casserole courtesy of Birds Eye Foods. Used with permission.

PAGE 73 Dole: Photo and recipe for Pineapple Chicken Packets courtesy of Dole Food Company. Used with permission.

PAGES 74/75 McCormick: Photo and recipe for Curried Chicken Potpie courtesy of McCormick. Used with permission.

PAGE 76 Sargento: Photo and recipe for Chicken Enchiladas courtesy of Sargento Foods Inc. Used with permission.

PAGE 77 Association of Dressings & Sauces: Recipe for Tostado Grande courtesy of The Association for Dressings & Sauces. Used with permission.

PAGE 78 Kraft Foods: Photo and recipe for Chicken Nuggets courtesy of Kraft Kitchens. Used with permission.

PAGE 79 American Egg Board: Recipe for Vichyssoise Tart courtesy the

American Egg Board. Used with permission.

PAGE 80 Sargento: Photo for Snapper Veracruz courtesy of Sargento Foods Inc. Used with permission.

PAGE 82 Kraft Foods: Recipe for Salmon with Tomatoes, Spinach & Mushrooms courtesy of Kraft Kitchens. Used with permission.

PAGE 83 Bruce Foods: Recipe for Crispy Oven Fish Bake courtesy of Bruce Foods Corporation. Used with permission.

PAGES 84/85 Catfish Institute: Photo and recipe for Catfish Parmesan courtesy of The Catfish Institute. Used with permission.

PAGE 86 Sargento: Photo and recipe for Snapper Veracruz courtesy of Sargento Foods Inc. Used with permission.

PAGE 87 Sunkist: Recipe for Lemon Trout courtesy of Sunkist Growers, Inc. Used with permission.

PAGE 88 Ocean Spray Cranberries: Recipe for Crab Meat in Phyllo Shells courtesy of Ocean Spray Cranberries, Inc. Used with permission.

PAGE 88 Birds Eye Foods: Recipe for Easy Fish & Vegetable Bake courtesy of Birds Eye Foods. Used with permission.

PAGE 89 Tone Brothers: Recipe for Fisherman's Wharf Crab Bake courtesy of Tone Brothers, Inc., producer of Tone's, Spice Islands, and Durkee products. Used with permission.

PAGES 90/91 Sargento: Photo and recipe for Acapulco Baked Fish courtesy of Sargento Foods Inc. Used with permission.

PAGE 92 Sunkist: Recipe for Crab & Artichoke Bake courtesy of Sunkist Growers, Inc. Used with permission.

PAGE 93 Zatarain's: Recipe for Shrimp Pie courtesy of Zatarain's. Used with permission.

PAGE 94 Kraft Foods: Photo for Boston Baked Beans courtesy of Kraft Kitchens. Used with permission.

PAGE 96 Tone Brothers: Recipe for Broccoli Cashew Casserole courtesy of Tone Brothers, Inc., producer of Tone's, Spice Islands, and Durkee products. Used with permission.

PAGE 97 Nestlé: Photo and recipe for Sweet Corn Pudding courtesy of Nestlé. All trademarks are owned by Société des Produits Nestlé S.A., Vevey, Switzerland. Used with permission.

PAGE 98 French's: Recipe for Double Cheddar Green Bean Casserole courtesy of French's® French Fried Onions. Used with permission.

PAGE 99 National Honey Board: Recipe for Honey Baked Red Onions courtesy of the National Honey Board. Used with permission.

PAGES 100/101 United States Potato Board: Recipe for Oven Roasted Potatoes courtesy of the United States Potato Board. Used with permission.

PAGE 102 French's: Recipe for Zippy Oven Fries courtesy of Frank's® RedHot®

Cayenne Pepper Sauce and French's® French Fried Onions. Used with permission.

PAGE 103 Sargento: Photo and recipe for Potatoes Au Gratin courtesy of Sargento Foods Inc. Used with permission.

PAGE 104 Kraft Foods: Recipe for Super Skins courtesy of Kraft Kitchens. Used with permission.

PAGE 105 Tone Brothers: Recipe for Yankee Sweet Potatoes courtesy of Tone Brothers, Inc., producer of Tone's, Spice Islands, and Durkee products. Used with permission.

PAGES 106/107 McCormick: Photo and recipe for Mashed Potato Bake courtesy of McCormick. Used with permission.

PAGE 108 National Pork Board: Recipe for Creamed Spinach courtesy of the National Pork Board. Used with permission.

PAGE 109 Florida Tomato Committee: Photo and recipe for Baked Tomatoes with Herb Topping courtesy of the Florida Tomato Commission. Used with permission.

PAGE 110 American Egg Board: Recipe for Twice Baked Squash courtesy of the American Egg Board. Used with permission.

PAGE 111 Sargento: Photo and recipe for Spinach Casserole courtesy of Sargento Foods Inc. Used with permission.

PAGE 112 Produce for Better Health Foundation: Recipe for Italian Vegetable Bake courtesy of Produce for Better Health Foundation. Used with permission.

PAGE 113 Kraft Foods: Photo and recipe for Boston Baked Beans courtesy of Kraft Kitchens. Used with permission.

PAGE 114 Uncle Ben's: Recipe for Cheese & Rice Soufflé courtesy of UNCLE BEN'S® Brand. Used with permission.

PAGE 115 Tone Brothers: Recipe for Irish Soda Bread courtesy of Tone Brothers, Inc., producer of Tone's Spice Islands, and Durkee Products. Used with permission.

PAGE 116 Kraft Foods: Recipe for Buttermilk Biscuits courtesy of Kraft Kitchens. Used with permission.

PAGE 117 Tone Brothers: Recipe for Pesto Bread courtesy fo Tone Brothers, Inc., producer of Tone's, Spice Islands, and Durkee products. Used with permission.

PAGE 118 Land O'Lakes: Photo and recipe for Savory Breadsticks courtesy of Land O'Lakes. Used with permission.

PAGE 119 Nestlé: Recipe for Corn Bread courtesy of Nestlé. All trademarks are owned by Société des Produits Nestlé S.A., Vevey, Switzerland. Used with permission.

PAGE 120 Dole: Photo for Banana Apple Betty courtesy of Dole Food Company. Used with permission.

PAGE 122 Produce for Better Health Foundation: Photo and recipe for Kiwifruit Cobbler courtesy of the Produce for Better Health Foundation. Used with permission.

PAGE 123 Birds Eye Foods: Recipe for Cherry Peach Cobbler courtesy of Birds Eye Foods. Used with permission.

PAGE 124 Tone Brothers: Recipe for Bread Pudding with Run Raisin Sauce courtesy of Tone Brothers, Inc., producer of Tone's, Spice Islands, and Durkee products. Used with permission.

PAGE 125 Tone Brothers: Recipe for Brandied Cherry Chocolate Bread Pudding with Vanilla Sauce courtesy of Tone Brothers, Inc., producer of Tone's, Spice Islands, and Durkee products. Used with permission.

PAGES 126/127 Dole: Recipe for Banana Apple Betty courtesy of Dole Food Company. Used with permission.

PAGE 128 Dole: Photo and recipe for Piña Colada Bread Pudding courtesy of Dole Food Company. Used with permission.

PAGE 129 Dole: Recipe for Caribbean Banana Cake courtesy of Dole Food Company. Used with permission.

PAGES 130/131 Dole: Recipe for Upside-Down Cake courtesy of Dole Food Company. Used with permission.

PAGE 132 The Sugar Association: Recipe for Sugar Lemon Squares courtesy of The Sugar Association. Used with permission.

PAGE 133 Cherry Marketing Institute: Photo and recipe for Very Cherry Pie courtesy of The Cherry Marketing Institute. Used with permission.

PAGE 134 The Sugar Association: Recipe for Stuffed Baked Apples courtesy of The Sugar Association. Used with permission.

PAGE 135 The Sugar Association: Recipe for Lemon Curd Tartlets courtesy of The Sugar Association. Used with permission.

PAGE 136 Dole: Photo and recipe for Banana Gingerbread Bars courtesy of Dole Food Company. Used with permission.

PAGE 137 American Egg Board: Recipe for Chocolate Sponge Custard courtesy of the American Egg Board. Used with permission.

PAGE 138 National Sunflower Association: Recipe for Apple Sunflower Strudel courtesy of the National Sunflower Association. Used with permission.

PAGE 139 American Egg Board: Recipe for Autumn Pumpkin Soufflé courtesy of the American Egg Board. Used with permission.

WEB SITES

RODALE INC.
www.rodale.com

American Egg Board
www.aeb.org

Association of Dressings and Sauces
www.dressings-sauces.org

B&G Foods
www.bgfoods.com

Birds Eye Foods
www.birdseyefoods.com

Bruce Foods
www.brucefoods.com

Bumble Bee
www.bumblebee.com

Catfish Institute
www.catfishinstitute.com

Cattlemen's Beef Board
www.beefitswhatsfordinner.com

Cherry Marketing Institute
www.usacherries.com

Del Monte
www.delmonte.com

Dole Food Company
www.dole.com

Florida Tomato Committee
www.floridatomatoes.org

French's
www.frenchsfoods.com

Kraft Foods
www.kraftfoods.com

Land O'Lakes, Inc.
www.landolakes.com

Mrs. T.'s Pierogies
www.pierogies.com

National Chicken Council
www.eatchicken.com

National Honey Board
www.honey.com

National Pasta Association
www.ilovepasta.org

National Pork Board
www.theotherwhitemeat.com

National Sunflowers Association
www.sunflowersna.com

Nestlé
www.meals.com

Ocean Spray Cranberries
www.oceanspray.com

Produce for Better Health Foundation
www.5aday.org

Quaker
www.quakeroats.com

Sargento
www.sargentocheese.com

The Sugar Association
www.sugar.org

Sunkist
www.sunkist.com

Tone Brothers
www.spiceadvice.com

Uncle Ben's
www.unclebens.com

United States Potato Board
www.potatohelp.com

Wisconsin Milk Marketing Board
www.wisdairy.com

Zatarain's
www.zatarain.com

INDEX

✔ Designates a SuperQuick recipe that gets you in and out of the kitchen in 30 minutes or less! **Boldface** page numbers refer to photographs. *Italicized* page numbers refer to boxed text.